A HARMONY OF

TWO
PSALMS

"In Guy Steward's work on *A Harmony of Two Psalms,* an exposition of Psalm 2 and Psalm 91, Guy powerfully demonstrates the reality that the Bible is, in the words of Chuck Missler, 'an integrated message system from outside of our time domain'. Guy draws on passages and themes from Genesis to Revelation to expand on the beautiful verses and themes found in these two outstanding Psalms. What has resulted is a journey that leads toward increased faith, trust, and confidence in a God Who, while existing outside of and beyond time, engages with those whose hearts are toward Him in interventions within time that are transformative and dynamic, even dramatic.

"My recommendation to you is to undertake this journey with simplicity of heart. God will reveal Himself as the One Who will interact with and care for you personally, as easily and specifically as He will in dealing with kings, rulers, and others in authority. I am enriched by reading Guy's insights, research, and integration of ideas. I know you will be also."

—Bruce McDonald
LIFT Ministries Trust

"Thank you for offering me the privilege of reading your beautiful book! I sensed the Spirit of God enhancing the wisdom of a deep relational interaction and 'kiss' with the eternal prophetic words of Psalms 2 and 91. The Messiah Christ Jesus shines brightly through the living words of the Almighty Author of the destiny of mankind! He makes himself so attractive that one can't help falling into passionate love with Him. Those who prosper will do so because they align their destiny with the revelation of the eternal purposes of the kingdom of God. I recommend this book to every passionate lover of Christ."

—Bryan A Johnson
CEO of The Asia Pacific Discipleship Trust CC28265
former Principal of New Covenant International Bible College
Auckland, New Zealand

A HARMONY OF

TWO
PSALMS

GUY ROBERT PEEL STEWARD

Ambassador International
GREENVILLE, SOUTH CAROLINA & BELFAST, NORTHERN IRELAND

www.ambassador-international.com

A Harmony of Two Psalms

ISBN: 978-1-64960-703-4
eISBN: 978-1-64960-717-1

Cover Design by Karen Slayne
Interior Typesetting by Dentelle Design
Edited by Katie Cruice Smith

All Scripture references are from the King James (Authorised) Version of the Bible. Public Domain.

AMBASSADOR INTERNATIONAL
Emerald House
411 University Ridge, Suite B14
Greenville, SC 29601
United States
www.ambassador-international.com

AMBASSADOR BOOKS
The Mount
2 Woodstock Link
Belfast, BT6 8DD
Northern Ireland, United Kingdom
www.ambassadormedia.co.uk

The colophon is a trademark of Ambassador, a Christian publishing company.

TABLE OF CONTENTS

PREFACE

IN TIMES OF CRISIS and change, people sometimes turn to Psalms such as Psalm 91 for security or comfort. Some see them as lucky charms to grab at when faced with sudden threats. However, while it is always dangerous to use Scriptures out of context, an equally egregious error is to dismiss them all as irrelevant and out-of-date or to decry their references to the "supernatural", which is really a different type of "natural". God, in eternity, exists outside our familiar timeframe and does not need to constantly send out new revelations. The Scriptures are enduring witnesses to His reality. Taking two key Psalms (2 and 91) for analysis and comparison, *A Harmony of Two Psalms* shows how such Scriptures relate to our daily walk with God, revealing our need to be aware of what He is saying to us today, along with the unique blessings of trusting Him. This can be approached as a word study, a devotional, or a thought-provoking read.

INTRODUCTION

GOD SPEAKS IN ALL the Psalms—through the voice of the writers, the events described, referred to, or inferred, and the emotions expressed. Whether the prophecies of Jesus (Whose voice is heard also occasionally in the Psalms, as in Psalm 2), King David's quoting God, or God Himself interjecting into the psalmist's free-verse poetry, all speak directly to us. In Psalm 2, God speaks from verse six on and in Psalm 91 from verse fourteen on. Although all the canon of Scripture is from God, those instances in which He speaks directly in a psalm are highly significant (see Psalm 50:7-23; 81:7-14; 82:6-7; 89:20-37; 95:8-11; and brief quotes in Psalm 27:8; 46:10; and 50:5, 15.)

Psalm 2 has four speakers; Psalm 91 has two. Psalm 2 is addressed to rulers such as kings and judges (by extension also presidents, prime ministers, politicians, mayors, etc.), and Psalm 91 is addressed to believers or prospective believers that they might live in the blessings of God. Psalm 2 is about the establishing of God's kingdom on earth through His Son's victory, and Psalm 91 is about the practical manifestation of that kingdom through the believer's faith. Psalm 2 has eschatological implications, Psalm 91 devotional. Both have four strophes. Both quote God verbatim. And both, in their final verse, point to the Lord Jesus Christ.

I encourage the memorisation of these psalms or at least familiarity with some of their verses. The translation we choose should be suitable for us personally so that we get the gist. I choose the King James Version here, also called the Authorised Version.[1] Regardless of its occasional weaknesses, it remains superb reading, coming as it does from an era when English Renaissance literature was at its height.

Divided into their six groups on three locations (Cambridge, Oxford, and Westminster), the translators of the King James Version, while not all "saints", were specialists in at least one or more of the ancient languages of Greek, Hebrew, Syriac, Aramaic, Arabic, and Latin. The Cambridge group which translated the first book of Chronicles through the Song of Solomon—and hence also the Psalms—was headed by Edward Lively, Regius Professor of Hebrew at Cambridge.

All translations have lyrical moments and the King James Version has many, despite some archaisms and awkward passages (such as the difficult verses in II Cor. 6:11-13). It often uses a language style no one would have spoken, even then in 1611. Naturally, lengthy genealogies such as Nehemiah 3, or tedious historical details, remain necessary whatever the translation. But while no translation is perfect, the King James Version is unlikely to ever be superseded. One of the reasons for that is its wealth of literary devices, plenty to satisfy any lover of first-rate literature.

Without debating which translation is best overall, I explore here that which works well. The rich figures of speech in the original languages were divinely inspired, and the translators did their utmost to render them faithfully. Their work also resulted in about two hundred idioms entering the English language.[2]

Since relatively few people now understand or read the ancient languages, we rely on translations, concordances, and dictionaries. A good reading experience is still important, however, so any translation that is as true as

---

1   Several excellent books on this translation are *Power and Glory* (2003) by Adam Nicholson, *Manifold Greatness: The Making of the King James Bible* (2011) by Helen Moore and Julian Reid, and *Begat* (2011) by David Crystal. Worthwhile, too, is the documentary, *KJV: The Making of the King James Bible,* (2011) written and directed by Jerry Griffith.

2   David Crystal, *Begat: The King James Bible and the English Language* (Oxford: Oxford University Press, 2011).

possible to the originals but also that has the message effectively packaged into the grammar, syntax, and lexicon of the target language is to be commended.

Use any translation as you study this, but allow yourself also to be fascinated by the poetic and prosaic beauty of the King James Version (*thees* and *thous* can be easily changed into *yous*).

Psalm 2 is an analysis. The second study, Psalm 91, ends with a restatement of the whole psalm. Several university papers on linguistics, some short SIL courses (Wycliffe Bible Translators), around twenty-five years of language teaching, and my own curiosity have all contributed towards this search into the Scripture's language use and origins. Basic exploration into the biblical languages and their connections also arose, for me, particularly from an interest in how God inspired the original Scriptures. However, digging into more complex grammar would require further study than what is necessary here, so I present only the basic forms of the Hebrew and Greek words and their derivations from dictionaries and concordances, plus occasional transliterations from resources such as Bible Hub and *The Blue Letter Bible*. Much is now freely available online. In general, I have found that the effort to comprehend the basics of language use is well worthwhile, even though time and other restrictions often limit our capacity to do further in-depth study.

I chose these two Psalms for two reasons: because they are outstanding examples of biblical literature and because they are relevant to world events. I seldom, however, attempt to link them to the latest headlines, since personal or national application is left to the reader. While in one sense self-explanatory, they need to be related first to the whole context of the book of Psalms (i.e., cross-referenced with other Psalms) and then to other Scripture. The theme highlighted is trust. Both Psalms affirm the maxim, "In God we trust."

The day before the first Covid-19-related lockdown in New Zealand in 2020, a colleague handed me a pocket-sized card with Psalm 91 written on it. At first impression, I considered it a thoughtful reminder of the need to trust God in such situations. I was prompted to take the challenge and explore the treasure of Psalm 91 (Prov. 2:4; Col. 2:3). So I began writing. Psalm 2's message, I found, also linked well with that of Psalm 91.

As an educator, I have always encouraged reading. The Psalms constitute a specific genre with literary value. However, the lack of depth of some modern English translations causes many people to find Bible reading difficult. Their aesthetic "literary senses" are left unsatisfied. We generally choose reading material with which we are comfortable, although we sometimes need a dictionary. And occasionally, we want only to skip through a text. Bible translations should encompass our reading experiences—simple ones for an overview or the general gist, referenced ones for insights into Hebrew and Greek, in-depth ones for a rich and enjoyable reading experience, or all of these. The original scripts were quality literature for focused reading, as well as God's mouthpiece—their *raison d'être*. Athanasius spoke of the eloquence of the original Scripture, and translations should also have some of the same.

The main literary devices used in the original languages, in many translations, in the King James Version, and in most good literature are as follows:

Alliteration

Alliteration indicates the repetition of the same sounds (especially initial consonants), generally with two or more words in succession. For example, in the book of Exodus we read, "Stand still, and see the salvation of the LORD" (Exod. 14:13; 15:16). And in Joshua 2:5, it is written, "Whither the men went I wot not". Also in Psalm 52:1, we read, "Why boastest thou thyself in mischief, O mighty man? the goodness of God endureth continually." And in Isaiah 27:6b, "Israel shall blossom and bud, and fill the face of the world with fruit."

From Psalm 104:3, we see a double metaphor: "Who walketh upon the wings of the wind". And in John 2, the translators seemed to have had a flurry of alliterative fun around *w* and *wh* and the word *wine*: "When they wanted wine"; "Woman, what have I to do with thee?"; "waterpots with water"; "When the ruler of the feast had tasted the water that was made wine, and knew not whence it was"; "good wine; and when men have well drunk, then that which is worse" (verses 3, 4, 7, 9, and 10). Examples abound also in the book of Job, such as, "The steps of his strength shall be straightened, and his own counsel shall cast him down" (18:7). Alliteration is used throughout the King James Version, although, as with all writing, some would have been unintentional.

Monosyllabicity

Another device used occasionally is monosyllabicity, which means that every word in a phrase and sometimes in a whole clause is one syllable, such as, "We know not with what we must serve the LORD" and "We wot not what" (Exod. 10:26; 32:1, both also using alliteration and rhyme), or "I wist not whence they were", (Josh. 2:4). We see it, too, in Job 2:10: "In all this did not Job sin with his lips" and in Mark 14:71: "I know not this man of whom ye speak."[3] [4]

Similes and Metaphors

A simile occurs when something is described by a comparison with another due to the resemblance that they both have (or will have). For example, in Moses' song in Exodus 15:11, we read that the enemies of Israel would end up being "as still as a stone" (with alliteration). Another is "the righteous shall flourish like the palm tree" (Psalm 92:12). The Bible is full of these; and if you glance through the Book of Job, the Psalms, the Proverbs, the Song of Solomon, and all the prophets, you will find many. Metaphors are a little different in that they involve naming the two directly as if they were one, such as "The LORD is my shepherd" (Psalm 23:1). The difference is that the Lord is not described as being *like* a shepherd (a simile) but that He *is* the Shepherd. Refer also to the examples under "Hyperbole" below.

3   *Literary Devices*, s.v. "Monosyllable", Accessed 23 March, 2017, https://literarydevices. net/monosyllable/.

4   Adam Sedia, "The Power of One: Monosyllables in Classical Poetry", The Society of Classical Poets, 18 February, 2021, https://classicalpoets.org/2021/02/18/the-power-of-onemonosyllables-in-classical-poetry/#/%20.

Hyperbole

This technique involves exaggeration for emphasis, often combined with metaphorical imagery, such as in Exodus 11:7: "But against any of the children of Israel shall not a dog move his tongue, against man or beast"; Leviticus 26:36: "The sound of a shaken leaf shall chase them" (with alliteration); "The land of your enemies shall eat you up" (Lev. 26:38); "Their tongue walketh through the earth" (Psalm 73:9); and "All the trees of the field shall clap their hands" (Isa. 55:12).

An example of a hyperbole, a simile, a metaphor, plus alliteration on the "s" sound, all providing an onomatopoeic[5] effect is, "They have sharpened their tongues like a serpent; adders' poison is under their lips. Selah" (Psalm 140:3). Other passages likewise combine such figures of speech, including alliteration, assonance (vowel rhyme), monosyllabicity, etc.

Chiasmi

This technique is in the original language. An example is, "And Moses wrote their goings out according to their journeys . . . and these are their journeys according to their goings out" (Num. 33:2).

Look again at the structure, and you will see how it works. Several parallel inversions are found in Exodus 30:10 and 32:15, but there are others. More on this to follow.

Discovering the real meaning behind figures of speech can be challenging at times, as in Psalm 121:6, where we read, "The sun shall not smite thee by day, nor the moon by night" or Proverbs 15:30, "The light of the eyes rejoiceth the heart: and a good report maketh the bones fat". Or try working out Ezekiel 13:20: "Behold, I am against your pillows,

---

5   Onomatopoeia occurs when words are formed to sound like what they are describing (e.g., the *hissing* of a snake).

wherewith ye there hunt the souls to make them fly", without some sort of external reference! To accurately discover the meaning of such phrases requires either proficiency in the ancient languages or, for most of us, an easier translation.

Allegory and Symbolism

Allegory and symbolism are also prominent in the Bible. For example, while "day" in Genesis 1 is not symbolic, "shadow" in Psalm 91:1 is (we do not literally *see* God's shadow). "Refuge", "fortress", "shield", and "buckler" are all easy-to-understand metaphors, while others such as "dragon" require further study. And others are even less clear. "Plague" or "pestilence", for example, could be literal, metaphorical (we refer to some non-biological annoyances as "pests" or "plagues"), or both. A plague or pestilence, however, is not a cold or a bout of mild flu but a greater danger, as is confirmed by the definitions and contexts of the words. God as our "Fortress" is symbolic, representing our response to His call, while words about trusting in God are *not* symbolic, for loving and calling on God involve genuine heart responses.

The Bible uses many other rhetorical devices such as analogies, parables, personifications, and types to describe physical *and* spiritual realities. And (at least in the KJV) archaic words such as "betimes" (Gen. 26:31), "yesternight" (Gen. 31:42), or "hungerbitten" (Job 18:12) provide further interest for us.

Psalms 2 and 91 employ both literal and figurative language, the literal usually being obvious and the figurative relatively easy to work out.

Parallelisms

Many verses in the Psalms employ parallelisms, including the following examples:

1. Synonymous parallelism— the first statement is echoed by the second but in different words, as in Psalm 119 or in Proverbs 15:30.

Synonymous parallelism can also be chiasmic, an example being Genesis 1:27a: "So God made man in his own image, in the image of God created he him". The meaning is identical for both clauses with aspects of the sentence structure and grammar changed (subject/ verb/object plus adverbial phrase in the first and adverbial phrase and verb/subject/object in the second).

2. Contrasting or antithetical parallelism—the first line is confirmed in the second by its opposite, as in Proverbs 14:30 and Psalm 91:12. This is also called reverse parallelism (or chiasmi, sing. chiasmus), where the meaning is reversed to prove the point, as in Psalm 1, Matthew 20:16a—"So the last shall be first, and the first last"—and Mark 2:27—"The sabbath was made for man, and not man for the sabbath" (for succinctness, the verb phrases in these two examples are only inferred in the second clauses).

3. Synthetical parallelism—the second theme is based on the first (i.e., cause and effect) as in Psalm 1:3. This is the most common type.

4. Ascending parallelism, also called climactic—the second statement (or statements) completes the first, as in Psalm 1:1.

5. Emblematic parallelism—a figurative phrase or clause is used to illustrate the meaning of the main (usually the first) statement, as in Psalm 1:4.

Two lines together make a couplet, but they could also be trebled or quadrupled.[6] [7] Doubling of ideas, words, phrases, and themes is common, starting from Genesis all throughout the Old Testament (Hebrew) and the New Testament (Greek). This use of twos as in parallelisms is for emphasis and is clearly seen in the two psalms considered in this book.

---

6   Technically named tercet and quatrain respectively.
7   E.g., John E. Worgul, "The Quatrain in Isaianic Poetry", *Grace Theological Journal* 11, no. 2 (1990): 187-204. https://biblicalstudies.org.uk/pdf/gtj/11-2_187.pdf.

Strophes

Strophes (stanzas) are divisions assigned to different themes or speakers in a poem, equivalent to paragraphs in prose, or verses, choruses, and bridges in songs.

Some may say that a study such as this makes too much of a simple text. However, although the message may be simple, these psalms contain vast riches to explore and enjoy. Nothing was included in a casual or haphazard way. As a language teacher, I have often had to "make much" of a piece of writing, dissecting texts for the sake of the students in consideration of the meaning, register, context, grammar, syntax, and use of those texts. Translators of Holy Scripture were God's instruments; and in ancient scribal tradition, those who produced our greatest versions were scholars to whom we are beholden for such literary treasures as these psalms.

It will be worthwhile to have your Bible beside you as you read through this book. Ultimately, God is the Author and Master Linguist. Studying these Scriptures can help us avoid unreasonable or extreme views. We stand in awe of them and approach them with reverence, not casually, not quoting them glibly, but seeking to understand them better. Any book about them can serve only as an introduction as we learn them and learn to live them.

PART ONE
PSALM 2

THE PLACE OF RULERS AND THE PLACE OF THE SAVIOUR

CHAPTER 1

INTRODUCTION TO PSALM 2

PSALM 2 IS HISTORICAL drama and a wonderful example of biblical literary style with its many doubles, parallelisms, and alliterations. Within twelve verses, it reveals the results of the Fall—global turmoil, social unrest, political conflict, and oppression—and God's reaction to ungodly rulers, plus the cross and the resurrection, the sovereignty of the Lord Jesus Christ, and instructions for how to prepare for His reign, all clearly related to Jesus, as the New Testament confirms.

A prayer by one of the earliest first century assemblies of believers, as recorded in the fourth chapter of the Acts of the Apostles, included its first two verses: "Who by the mouth of thy servant David hast said, Why did the heathen rage, and the people imagine vain things? The kings of the earth stood up, and the rulers were gathered together against the Lord, and against his Christ" (4:25-26). This assembly or "company" of the apostles Peter and John clearly knew who the author of the psalm was. Whether it had previously been considered to have been anonymously written or compiled by scribes, as with Psalm 1 for instance, this one—Psalm 2—came from "the mouth" of God's servant, David. The context of the prayer was a time of persecution of the newly-born Jerusalem church, persecution coming from both Israel and the "Gentiles" in Jerusalem at the time.

The persecutors are recorded as being:

Priests, and the captain of the temple, and the Sadducees . . . their rulers, and elders, and scribes, And Annas the high priest, and Caiaphas, and John, and Alexander, and as many as were of the kindred of the high priest . . . gathered together at Jerusalem . . . rulers of the people, and elders of Israel . . . the chief priests and elders . . . both Herod, and Pontius Pilate, with the Gentiles, and the people of Israel (Acts 4:1, 5, 6, 8, 23, 27).

All these religious rulers, Israelite and non-Israelite, were gathered together against God's "holy child Jesus, whom thou hast anointed" (v. 27).

So, does Psalm 2 have application outside of this context? Did it apply at the time it was written by David the king, prophet, and scribe? Can we be sure it applies to Jesus? Could it have had application at any other time in the last two thousand years? And could it apply today? The answer to all these questions is yes.

Let us start with what God said: "Yet have I set my king upon my holy hill of Zion" (v. 6). "I have set" was written approximately a thousand years before Jesus. But God calls "those things which be not as though they were" (Rom. 4:17). So the verse—and therefore, the whole psalm—is prophetic first of the monarchy of Israel, then of Jesus, and third of His people (the called-out ones[8]). All of this originated in eternity, as God's Divine intention.

Second is the application to David. David was God's anointed son (I Sam. 16:13); and even before becoming king, he had practice ruling—in the spirit of Psalm 2:9—in his victories over a lion, a bear, and then Goliath (I Sam. 17:34ff). He later ruled from the holy hill of Zion (II Sam. 5:7; I Kings 8:1) and numerous other times defeated the enemies of Israel (e.g., II Sam. 5:17-25).

To Solomon, David's son, God stated that his throne would be established upon Israel forever (II Sam. 7:12-16; I Kings 9:5), and we see New Testament fulfilment of this in the Lord Jesus Christ, Who was "of the seed of David according to the flesh" (Rom. 1:3) and Who Himself said He was "the root and

---

8   W.E. Vine, *An Expository Dictionary of New Testament Words*, s.v. "ekklēsia" (Iowa Falls: Riverside Book and Bible House, 1952), 75, 220.

the offspring of David" (Rev. 22:16). Certainly, then, it applied to Jesus as well as to the Davidic line of kings.

Let us see if the psalm might apply to any other king. To illustrate, we can consider an incident in the reign of King Hezekiah (a generally good king and well down the line from David) when he was assailed around 691-688 B.C. by King Sennacherib in the second of his campaigns against Israel. Sennacherib, whose father was Sargon, was the most famous—or rather notorious—of Assyria's kings. Remember the main themes of the psalm: the raging heathen, kings and rulers, laughter from God sitting in Heaven, God's wrath, the request to God by His Son, and the breaking of the enemies, the whole series of events being instructive to rulers to respect and serve God.

What was the unexpected result—keeping in mind that Israel was under the Assyrian yoke of terror at the time? According to the story found in Isaiah 37 and II Kings 18 and 19, Sennacherib had sent his official, Rabshakeh, to intimidate and warn Israel of impending invasion and defeat, which amounted to reproaching God, as Hezekiah's message to the prophet Isaiah stated. Hezekiah commanded a response of silence to Rabshakeh's threats but took his cause to Isaiah, who prophesied accordingly.

Hezekiah then prayed (i.e., "ask of me"), and as a result God spoke of how the people had derided Sennacherib: "The virgin, the daughter of Zion, hath despised thee, and laughed thee to scorn; the daughter of Jerusalem hath shaken her head at thee" (Isa. 37:22). And then, because Sennacherib's rage against God came up into His ears (v. 29), God said, "I will defend this city to save it for mine own sake, and for my servant David's sake" (v. 35). Then God destroyed the Assyrian army by sending an angel to kill 185,000 of them, and in 689 B.C. Sennacherib's two sons murdered him, as Isaiah had prophesied.

We can see how Psalm 2 was partially fulfilled, played out as part of the heritage of Israel's monarchy. Not everything fits perfectly, of course—the people of Jerusalem, not God, were laughing, and God Himself effected the victory, Hezekiah and Israel being in too desperate a state to be able to do it themselves. But the legacy of the promise to David, however dim, was there.

Psalm 2 has application also over the last two thousand years until today, and its greatest fulfilment remains in Jesus. Undoubtedly the initial and main context is in the above-mentioned prayer from the fourth chapter of Acts and then throughout the book of Acts. Jesus had risen from the dead and given His disciples and followers their commission (Matt. 28:18-20; Acts 1:8). The Church began, and so did the persecution—and with it the challenge from Psalm 2 to the persecutors, to all rulers and judges, to "be wise", to "be instructed", to "serve the LORD", and to "kiss the Son", as was customary for respect and friendship (vv. 10-12). And all were told to "put their trust in him" (v. 12).

But it did not end with Acts, for that was only the beginning. It continued with the establishment and training of the early churches, the destruction in A.D. 70 of Jerusalem, which itself was broken "with a rod of iron" and dashed into pieces "like a potter's vessel", (v. 9), and the continuation of God's work throughout the last two millennia. This also involves the possession of the "inheritance" and "the uttermost parts of the earth" through Jesus' intervention and through the power of the Holy Spirit working in and through His Church. It has been going throughout history, has not stopped, and will not stop until all things are under His feet (I Cor. 15:25), however and whenever that takes place.

The structure for Psalm 2 is laid out as Strophe One (vv. 1-3), Strophe Two (vv. 4-6), Strophe Three (vv. 7-9), and Strophe Four (vv. 10-12).

Strophe One

Verse one is a question in two parts, referring to two groups of people not dissimilar from each other (the heathen and the people): "Why do the heathen rage, and the people imagine a vain thing?"

Verse two describes two groups of people in authority (kings and rulers) and two entities they oppose (the LORD and His anointed): "The kings of the earth set themselves, and the rulers take counsel together, against the LORD, and against his anointed, saying".

Verse three then relates two statements by the kings and rulers: "Let us break their bands asunder, and cast away their cords from us".

Strophe Two

Verse four provides two statements of God's reaction to the people mentioned in Strophe One: "He that sitteth in the heavens shall laugh: the Lord shall have them in derision."

Verse five tells us what God says and what He does: "Then shall he speak unto them in his wrath, and vex them in his sore displeasure".

Verse six reveals God's accomplished plan: "Yet have I set my king upon my holy hill of Zion".

Strophe Three

Strophe Three shows Jesus' response. Verse seven is Jesus' declaration of what God has told Him: "I will declare the decree: the Lord hath said unto me, Thou art my Son; this day have I begotten thee".

Then in verse eight, Jesus' quote from God is continued, revealing God's invitation and intention: "Ask of me, and I shall give thee the heathen for thine inheritance, and the uttermost parts of the earth for thy possession".

Finally, verse nine gives us two statements of what Jesus does to deal with the rebellion: "Thou shalt break them with a rod of iron; thou shalt dash them in pieces like a potter's vessel".

Strophe Four

Strophe Four wraps up the psalm by showing the reader God's will: verse ten beginning with two of His injunctions to rulers: "Be wise now therefore,

O ye kings: be instructed, ye judges of the earth", verse eleven giving two more commandments to rulers: "Serve the Lord with fear, and rejoice with trembling", and verse twelve concluding the psalm with another bid to rulers, followed by a warning, and then a beatitude for those who trust God: "Kiss the Son, lest he be angry, and ye perish from the way, when his wrath is kindled but a little. Blessed are all they that put their trust in him".

To summarize, two types of authority are contrasted in this psalm: God's authority—benevolent but powerful—and man's—puny and rebellious. Two entities (v. 1) are affected by two other entities (v. 2a), declaring two utterances (v. 3) against another two (v. 2b). God's response is fourfold (vv. 4-6). His gift to His Son is twofold (v. 8), and the Son's commission includes two powerful actions (v. 9). Five commands are given (vv. 10-12a), and the psalm is wrapped up with a truism, a beatitude (v. 12b).

CHAPTER 2
QUESTION, COLLUSION, CONSPIRACY

STROPHE ONE

"Why do the heathen rage, and the people imagine a vain thing?" (v. 1)

OTHER WRITERS[9] HAVE NOTED the fact that this psalm precedes the "Hallelujah Chorus" in Handel's *Messiah*. While everyone knows the "Hallelujah Chorus", less well-known are the previous seven to eight minutes of excerpts from Psalm 2, which help set the scene for that wonderful chorus.

Handel's narrative begins with the first two verses and goes on to include a quivering recitative illustrating the words of the rebels encouraging each other to "break their bands asunder, and cast away their cords from us". The libretto uses aria and that naturally restless recitative to musically present verses one through four and nine.

Why did Handel do this? Why place Psalm 2 before the "Hallelujah Chorus"? Studying it reveals why the verses chosen formed such a good introduction to the declaration of the King of kings and Lord of lords reigning forever and ever.

The first word in this psalm is why. Psalms 10 and 52 begin the same way. And other interrogative introductions are found throughout the Psalms: "LORD, how" (Psalm 3); "How long" (Psalm 13); and "O God, why" (Psalm 74).

---

9   E.g., Gordon Wenham, *The Psalter Reclaimed: Praying and Praising with the Psalms.* (Wheaton, Illinois: Crossway, 2013).

But whereas those are all personal cries from the psalmist or the people of Israel to God, this question in Psalm 2 seems to be a leading one, perhaps even from God, taking us into the heart of why the world is in its current state. The question could also be rhetorical and exclamatory, as in, "Why do they do that which is unnecessary and futile? How can they fight against God?" Nevertheless, we cannot leave the question unanswered.

Why do people rebel against God and His ways? The word preceding "rage" in verse one is the usual noun *gôyim*,[10] denoting heathen nations both near and far from ancient Israel but also, in both positive and negative ways, Israel itself[11]. The word could also be used for a troop of animals or a flight of locusts, the idiomatic similarities being apt here with a picture of unsettled nations.

"Rage", in the original language, sounds onomatopoeic[12]. "People" refers to a likeminded group of people, referring, in the first case, to ungodly nations surrounding ancient Jerusalem and Israel but also, more widely, to communities of people confused and distressed, furious at being oppressed, or who have leaders who oppose God.

And they are considering "a vain thing"—a thing of no value. The word "vain" speaks of emptiness or worthlessness[13], as in Leviticus 26:16b: "Ye shall sow your seed in vain", and verse 20a: "Your strength shall be spent in vain". And "imagine" reveals *why* they might be raging, carrying for us a picture of them considering their complaints and murmuring amongst themselves[14]. (The word is also used positively in Psalm 1, referring to the godly individual who meditates in—or mutters—God's Word day and night.)

In Psalm 2, the masses are first complaining, angry, dismayed, discontented, rioting, rebelling, worrying, and scheming. Second, they

---

10   James Strong, *Strong's Expanded Exhaustive Concordance of the Bible* (Nashville: Thomas Nelson, 1990), s.v. "gôyim," 26.
11   E.g., "I will make of thee a great nation" (Gen. 12:2a), or "Ah sinful nation" (Isa. 1:4a).
12   Strong, s.v. "râgash," 107.
13   Strong, s.v. "rîyq," 108.
14   Strong, s.v. "hagah," 32.

are fussing, muttering, and murmuring about fruitless, ineffectual, and insignificant matters. A contemporary parallel is modern media, which often occupies itself and its subscribers with issues that, apart from essential news, are mundane and unimportant—especially in the light of eternity. Yet the fretting of the people could be related also to the emptiness of their lives, made even emptier and more worthless by those who rule over them.

"Vanish", "vain", and "vanity" in English all have the same Latin root—*vānus*, empty or without substance.[15] The people's dissatisfaction is cunningly exploited by their leaders' specifically setting themselves up against God, as we shall see in the next two verses. As Alexander Maclaren stated in his *The Book of Psalms: Volume I*, "Plot and strive, conspire and muster, as men may, all is vanity and striving of wind".[16]

Therefore, "Why do the heathen rage, and the people imagine a vain thing?" seems not to be rhetorical as much as a call for answers. Psalm 2, though having initial application for its time, relates also to the present and the future. Uprisings and riots of questionable legitimacy, crowds committing random violence and destruction, masses chasing after useless interests, frustrated, hurting, and concerned people sometimes led astray because of their rulers' stance against God are all implied by this verse.

But so far, we have not been given the answer to the question; so we too ask, "Why?"

In verses two and three we get the answer: "The kings of the earth set themselves, and the rulers take counsel together, against the LORD, and against his anointed, saying, Let us break their bands asunder, and cast away their cords from us" (vv. 2, 3).

---

15   T. F. Hoad, ed., *The Concise Oxford Dictionary of Word Origins*, (Oxford: Oxford University Press, 1986), 519.

16   Alexander MacLaren, "Psalm 2", Blue Letter Bible, Last Modified 15 April 2022, https://www.blueletterbible.org/comm/maclaren_alexander/the-expositors-bible/psalms-volume-one/psalm-two.cfm.

Here in these three sets of couplets in verses two and three is the reason for the unrest. The rulers have arraigned themselves in league against God and have irresponsibly misled or stirred up the people. Evidence of collusion against God's appointed Ruler and His chosen people leaps out in glaringly obvious ways throughout history. These verses clearly express the unmitigated, implacable hatred emanating from those who plot and plan the downfall of others out of abhorrence of God. These are both the organised representatives of and the sovereigns over the people of verse one.

This passage speaks of rebellion even more than the first. In answer to verse one's question, here is stated the cause for the heathens' raging and the people's murmuring. In their sinfulness, they have either rejected the Divine One or, lost without good leadership, have focused their anger on institutions, traditions, and leaders. Some may be angry with God, too. While we cannot dismiss the possibility—applicable in many instances—of *both* groups being united against the Lord and His anointed, the focus from this point forward is not as much on the people of verse one—the raging and deceived masses—as on those of verse two, the kings and rulers (the *them* of verses four and five) who, unyielding to God, are the cause. The psalm concentrates on them, and to them are the final five instructions mainly directed.

To those declaring the two defiant utterances in verse three ("Let us break their bands asunder, and cast away their cords from us"), the prophet Isaiah would have aimed his judgement: "Woe unto them that decree unrighteous decrees" (Isa. 10:1a).

The people follow their kings and rulers, and both groups set themselves against God, the former (the people) being the disorganised version, the latter the organised. The rulers and kings "set" themselves. "Set" here has the sense of strong determination, of standing fast. It indicates a stubborn resolve. Other instances that illustrate it in a positive sense include:

- "I will stand upon my watch, and set me upon the tower, and will watch to see what he will say unto me, and what I shall answer when I am reproved" (Hab. 2:1).
- "And they set themselves in the midst of that parcel [of ground], and delivered it, and slew the Philistines; and the LORD saved them by a great deliverance" (I Chron. 11:14).

The Aramaic equivalent for "set" is in Daniel 7:19a and is only there (chapters two to seven of Daniel being written in Aramaic) where it refers to being certain about a matter: "Then I would know the truth[17] of the fourth beast". Daniel was determined to know the meaning about the fourth beast in his vision of four beasts representing four kings. This fourth, which was to "devour the whole earth, and . . . tread it down, and break it in pieces" (v. 23. Viz., the "beast" of Rev. 13:1, 2, 11; 11:7; 17:8) had ten horns (v. 24; Rev. 17:12), the chief of which, according to Daniel:

> made war with the saints, and prevailed against them [cf. Rev. 11:7; 13:7]; Until the Ancient of days came, and judgment was given to the saints of the most High: and the time came that the saints possessed the kingdom. . . . But the judgement shall sit [cf. Rev. 20:4], and they shall take away his dominion, to consume and to destroy it unto the end. And the kingdom and dominion, and the greatness of the kingdom under the whole heaven, shall be given to the people of the saints of the most High, whose kingdom is an everlasting kingdom, and all dominions shall serve and obey him. (Dan. 7:21-22, 26-27; cf. Rev. 11:15)

We will hear much more of this "most High" in our study of Psalm 91.

Revelation 11:15 heralds that "Hallelujah Chorus"! "The kingdoms of this world are become the kingdoms of our Lord, and of his Christ; and he shall reign for ever and ever".

---

17   Strong, s.v. "yetsêb," 51.

So we see the determination of these ungodly leaders of Psalm 2:2 to "take counsel together"[18], sitting down and consulting with each other, plotting and conspiring in unity. Psalm 31:13 also uses it: "They took counsel together against me." And we see parallel language in Psalm 83:1-5. All this rebellion is ultimately against God.

Who is, or are, the "anointed"? In the first instance, as seen above, it is the king of ancient Israel. But because this psalm is one of the most quoted in the New Testament, no Christian could stop at interpreting it solely as a king who lived more than three thousand years ago, as doing so would invalidate the New Testament passages.

This verse and verse nine are repeated three times each in the New Testament. We have also seen that God's "anointed"—while first David or his line such as Solomon of whom God said, "I will be his father, and he shall be my son" (II Sam. 7:14)—is also Jesus and God's people, a prophecy of multiple fulfilment. The "anointed"[19] indicates God visible as the Messiah and comes from the word for to anoint or consecrate. According to the New Testament, then, the implication of the rebellion is that it is against God, His consecrated Son, and also the Holy Spirit, Who does the anointing.

The couplet in verse two, with its two instances of onomatopoeic alliteration (break, bands/cast, cords),[20] reveals that first, the conspiracy is not a secret but is out there, obvious, overt, flagrant, in-your-face, in God's face. They are saying, "Let us break away from the Divine influence!"

Cords are what Samson was bound with, as we read in Judges 15:13-14, but which, when the Spirit of God came upon him, became "flax that was burnt with fire" and were easily broken. And God said that He would "cut asunder the cords of the wicked" (Psalm 129:4) which they put upon others (Psalm 140:5). The kings and rulers of Psalm 2 were also held by the cords of their

---

18   Strong, s.v. "yâçad," 50.
19   Strong, s.v. "mâshîyah," 74.
20   ABC: "**A**gainst his Anointed"; "**B**reak their Bands"; "**C**ast away their Cords" (a useful mnemonic).

own sins (Prov. 5:22), and those are bands and cords that God can cut (Psalm 107:14; Jer. 2:20). But the "bands" and "cords" of verse three represent God's constraints against sin, which He gave to His people and, through His laws, to us all for our benefit. They were there in His commandments to Adam and Eve and to Israel but have always been onerous to those who choose not to love Him. Today, haters of God's laws continue to conspire, despising constraints and hankering for "freedom" to do what *they* wish and not what He wishes. And because sin rules and dominates them, they, in turn, desire to dominate others.

But this longing to overthrow God and His anointed—and their rule—is short-lived. God's "bands" and "cords" (as perceived by those in rebellion) can never be broken; rather, individuals and nations break themselves upon His laws. Indeed, "the haters of the LORD should have submitted themselves unto him" (Psalm 81:15a). An appeal for them to do so is coming later in this psalm.

CHAPTER 3

MIRTH, MOCKERY, FURY, ACTION

STROPHE TWO

"He that sitteth in the heavens shall laugh:
the Lord shall have them in derision." (v. 4)

AGAIN, WE HAVE A couplet. The verb phrases are "sitteth", "shall laugh", and "shall have them in derision". Here, circumstances have changed. The joke has fallen on the mockers. A feature of those who resist God and His ways is derision. Why, then, should they be surprised if God returns it? Yet while theirs is through petty spite, His is from the position of One Who sees it all as both tragic *and* laughable.

The opposite of hate is love, but equally, the opposite of vitriol can be mirth. If God is loving to all, then this might be considered a problem, even ludicrous; but the idea of Divine laughter is hyperbolic, a metaphor, a euphemism for when the tables are turned. While God is upholding those who place their love on Him—as we will also read about in Psalm 91:14—He does not take seriously the pathos and foolishness of the ungodly. Ironically, it becomes a "time to laugh" (Eccl. 3:4). And while doing so, He is seated. The first verse of Psalm 91 will show us how we also may sit (the same word) together with Him in His secret place.

The "laugh" and "derision" words in Hebrew are both onomatopoeic[21] [22]. The word for "derision" is elsewhere translated "laugh" (as in Job 9:23; 22:19; and Psalm 80:6). And Psalm 2's word for "laugh" is also found in Psalm 37:13: "The Lord shall laugh at him: for he seeth that his day is coming". Even God's people have their moment of this: "The righteous also shall see, and fear, and shall laugh at him" (Psalm 52:6). Psalm 59:8 has both words: "Thou, O LORD, shalt laugh at them; thou shalt have all the heathen in derision". And the same words are again found in Proverbs 1:26, where God laughs at those who have rejected all His counsel: "I also will laugh at your calamity; I will mock when your fear cometh".

We will see this fear mentioned in Proverbs 1:26, described as "terror" in Psalm 91:5. Fear will come to those who love evil more than good and lying rather than speaking righteousness (Psalm 52:3). For God will "destroy thee for ever, he shall take thee away, and pluck thee out of thy dwelling place, and root thee out of the land of the living" (Psalm 52:5). Asaph mused on the fate of the foolish and the end of the wicked, "How are they brought into desolation, as in a moment! They are utterly consumed with terrors" (Psalm 73:19).

Why is God depicted in Proverbs 1:26 as mocking? "Because I have called, and ye refused; I have stretched out my hand, and no man regarded" (Prov. 1:24).

We come to yet another couplet in verse five of the psalm, with the verbs "speak" and "vex": "Then shall he speak unto them in his wrath, and vex them in his sore displeasure" (v. 5).

The laughter has now ceased. God has had enough. Consequently, He now speaks in "wrath",[23] a word found also in verse twelve, and vexes them. The rulers vex their subjects, so God vexes them. Vex is followed by "sore displeasure", which would be read today as an understatement for "holy anger". It is derived from the Latin *vexāre* (to shake or disturb), connected

---

21   Strong, s.v. "sâchaq," 114.
22   Strong, s.v. "la'ag," 60.
23   Strong, s.v. "'âph," 15.

with *veho* and *vectum* (to carry), from which we get words like *vehicle* or *vector*. This descriptive word's meanings range from slightly bothering or irritating others through petty annoyances, to grieving, distressing, or plaguing them.

God annoys rulers who think they are supreme—sending them constant hassles and irritations—because they have to learn that life does not go smoothly when they do wrong. In His timing, He also grieves, distresses, and plagues them for the same reasons. The consequences then can go from light to mild to severe. "Woe unto them that decree unrighteous decrees, and that write grievousness which they have prescribed; To turn aside the needy from judgment, and to take away the right from the poor of my people, that widows may be their prey, and that they may rob the fatherless!" (Isa. 10:1-2).

God is right to vex the kings and rulers who try to break the bands of His laws and cast away the cords of His ways. Is it because He is capricious and changeable—happy one minute and angry the next? No, that is how rulers such as Pharaoh were and are. For God knows that kings and rulers are often also oppressors in the tradition of Egypt's pharaohs. They promise freedom and then withdraw it—promising and withdrawing, promising and withdrawing. "So I returned, and considered all the oppressions that are done under the sun: and behold the tears of such as were oppressed, and they had no comforter; and on the side of their oppressors there was power; but they had no comforter" (Eccl. 4:1). And if those oppressors claim their right from the Creator, the question needs to be asked, "Shall the throne of iniquity have fellowship with thee, which frameth mischief by a law?" (Psalm 94:20). Of course, the answer is no. They cannot "have fellowship" with God.

What then to do? "If thou seest the oppression of the poor, and violent perverting of judgment and justice in a province, marvel not at the matter: for he that is higher than the highest regardeth" (Eccl. 5:8). God looks on. And in His time, He moves as His people intercede, crying, "It is time for thee, LORD, to work: for they have made void thy law" (Psalm 119:126).

So what does He do to those who have violated and disannulled His law? First, He stands up and pleads for His people (Isa. 3:13), saying, "What mean ye that ye beat my people to pieces, and grind the faces of the poor?" (Isa. 3:15). Then He acts. "Yet have I set my king upon my holy hill of Zion." (v. 6)

Here in verse six, God now speaks for the first time in this psalm. He speaks of what He has already done. In anticipation of the need, He has set His king on His holy hill of Zion (cf. Rev. 14:1).

"Set" here is not the same as the standing fast of the kings who set themselves against God in verse two. In verse six, "set" means pouring out by anointing. And anointing is appointing! God has appointed a king (as in verse two). "Holy" refers to a sacred place—in this case "Zion"[24] (a word which includes the idea of being conspicuous)—hence, a noticeable place of special religious importance. "Hill" can also mean a range of hills.

Traditionally, Zion was the "Jebus" taken by David from the Jebusites on the south-eastern hill of Jerusalem, not the present Mount Zion on the southwest. Zion was also called the city of David, as in its first mention in II Samuel 5:7. The temple was built above this hill, and the whole area was later named Zion. Over time, the word became synonymous with the whole city of Jerusalem and its people ("the daughter of Zion"—e.g., Isa. 1:8; Jer. 4:31). Its main meaning, though, was as a figure of speech for God's dwelling place—a line which can be traced through the Exodus, the tabernacle, the temple, Jesus, the Church, the temple in Heaven, and the New Jerusalem—as shown below with the pertinent Scriptures, following the theme of "cloud" and "glory"—and sometimes "smoke" and "fire"—from Exodus to Revelation:

I. The Exodus and Mount Sinai
- "The LORD went before them by day in a pillar of a cloud, to lead them the way; and by night in a pillar of fire, to give them

---

24   Strong, s.v. "Tsîyôwn," 99.

light . . . the glory of the LORD appeared in the cloud." (Exod. 13:21; 16:10b)

- "The glory of the LORD abode upon Mount Sinai, and the cloud covered it six days . . . and the sight of the glory of the LORD was like devouring fire." (Exod. 24:16a, 17)

2. The Tabernacle

- "There I will meet with the children of Israel, and the tabernacle shall be sanctified by my glory." (Exod. 29:43)
- "Then a cloud covered the tent of the congregation, and the glory of the LORD filled the tabernacle . . . the cloud of the LORD was upon the tabernacle by day, and fire was on it by night." (Exod. 40:34, 38a)
- "I will appear in the cloud upon the mercy seat." (Lev. 16:2)
- "On the day that the tabernacle was reared up the cloud covered the tabernacle . . . and at even there was upon the tabernacle as it were the appearance of fire, until the morning." (Num. 9:15ff)

3. The Temple

- "Then Solomon . . . [brought] the ark of the covenant of the LORD [containing the two tables of the Ten Commandments] out of the city of David, which is Zion . . . into the most holy place [the Jerusalem temple] . . . when they . . . praised the LORD . . . the house was filled with a cloud . . . so that the priests could not stand to minister by reason of the cloud: for the glory of the LORD had filled the house of God." (II Chron. 5:2, 7, 13-14)
- "Fill thine hand with coals of fire from between the cherubims . . . and the house was filled with the cloud, and the court was full of the brightness of the LORD's glory." (Ezek. 10:2, 4)
- "I will fill this house with glory." (Hag. 2:7b)

And prophetically, while also hearkening back to the tabernacle:

- "And the LORD will create upon every dwelling place of mount Zion, and upon her assemblies, a cloud and smoke by day, and the shining of a flaming fire by night: for upon all the glory shall be a defence. And there shall be a tabernacle for a shadow in the daytime from the heat, and for a place of refuge, and for a covert from storm and from rain." (Isa. 4:5, 6; cf. Psalm 91:2, 9)

4. Jesus

- "A bright cloud overshadowed them." (Matt. 17:5—the Transfiguration)
- "They saw his glory." (Luke 9:32—the Transfiguration)
- "They shall see the Son of man coming in the clouds of heaven with power and great glory." (Matt. 24:30b)
- "Then shall they see the Son of man coming in a cloud with power and great glory." (Luke 21:27)[25]
- "The Lord Jesus shall be revealed from heaven with his mighty angels, In flaming fire . . . the glory of his power." (II Thess. 1:7b – 9)
- "When the LORD shall build up Zion, he shall appear in his glory." (Psalm 102:16)
- "To him be glory and dominion . . . Behold he cometh with clouds." (Rev. 1:6b, 7a)
- "A Lamb stood on the mount Sion." (Revelation 14:1a)

5. The Church:

- "He shall baptize you with the Holy Ghost, and with fire." (Matt. 3:11)
- "Ye shall receive power . . . and a cloud received him out of their sight." (Acts 1:8a, 9b)
- "There came a sound from heaven as of a rushing mighty wind . . . cloven tongues like as of fire, and it sat upon each of them." (Acts 2:2a, 3)

---

25   Notice the alliterations of this verse: "see/Son", "coming/cloud", "great/glory".

- "Unto him be glory in the church by Christ Jesus throughout all ages" (Eph. 3:21)
- "Then we which are alive and remain shall be caught up together with them in the clouds, to meet the Lord in the air, and so shall we ever be with the Lord." (I Thess. 4:17)
- "When he shall come to be glorified in his saints." (II Thess. 1:10a)
- "The spirit of glory and of God resteth upon you." (I Pet. 4:14)

6. The Temple of God in Heaven

A. Portrayed in the Old Testament:

- "I saw also the Lord sitting upon a throne, high and lifted up, and his train filled the temple . . . the whole earth is full of his glory . . . and the house was filled with smoke." (Isa. 6:1, 3b, 4b)

B. Portrayed in the New Testament:

- "And I saw as it were a sea of glass mingled with fire . . . and, behold, the temple of the tabernacle of the testimony in heaven was opened . . . And the temple was filled with smoke from the glory of God, and from his power." (Rev. 15:2a, 5, 8a)

7. The New Jerusalem:

- "The holy city, new Jerusalem . . . the tabernacle of God is with men, and he will dwell with them . . . Having the glory of God . . . And the city had no need of the sun, neither of the moon, to shine in it: for the glory of God did lighten it, and the Lamb is the light thereof." (Rev. 21:2, 3, 11, 23)[26]

How this relates to us is found in the following verses:

- "Those that be planted in the house of the LORD shall flourish in the courts of our God". (Psalm 92:13)

---

26 Here, the clouds and the smoke are gone.

- "I am like a green olive tree in the house of God". (Psalm 52:8a)
- "Abide in me, and I in you". (John 15:4)

This "Zion", used extensively in the Psalms (thirty-seven times) and even more so in the Prophets, particularly Isaiah, is spelled "Sion" in the New Testament in its seven occurrences. We have seen then some of its provenance and development in the themes of clouds and glory, smoke and fire—tracked through Israel, the tabernacle and the city of David, the Jerusalem temple, Jesus, the Church, the temple of God in Heaven, and the new Jerusalem (Gal. 4:26, Heb. 12:22).

CHAPTER 4

DECREE, DIALOGUE, DISRUPTION

STROPHE THREE

"I will declare the decree: the Lord hath said unto me, Thou art my Son; this day have I begotten thee. Ask of me, and I shall give thee the heathen for thine inheritance, and the uttermost parts of the earth for thy possession. Thou shalt break them with a rod of iron; thou shalt dash them in pieces like a potter's vessel." (vv. 7-9)

VERSES SEVEN AND EIGHT have six rhymes on the "ee" sound ("decree", "me", "thee", etc.). The verb "declare"[27] was also used as the Hebrew noun for the ancient scribes of Israel. In English we have parallel words such as "cipher" and "decipher".

The speaker could be David making this initial statement, "I will declare the decree". Or it could be God continuing from verse six, stating first the decree that points us to the story of redemption, beginning with Jesus' words, "The LORD hath said unto me", and then Jesus' quote of God's most important statement of Who He is (God's Son). Or, perhaps more plausibly it is Jesus Himself stating, "I will declare the decree: the Lord hath said unto me", and then quoting what the Lord had in fact said to Him about Who He was, what He should ask, and what He would do, through to the end of verse nine. Jesus

---

27   Strong, s.v. "çâphar," 84.

(or God the Father) then delivers specific instructions for kings and judges—and us—in the last three verses.

Either way, this declaration, a verbal announcement, was written down for us for all time. God wrote it not only here but in its three reappearances in the New Testament. "Decree" means an enactment or a law. In declaring it, God is writing "in stone" what is permanent and eternal: "Thou art my Son; this day have I begotten thee".

The verse would mean nothing more than that the *earthly* king was God's "son", as in II Samuel 7:14a, through being anointed and appointed to be the king of Israel—and some read it *only* this way—were it not for the fact that it could never be solely interpreted as such by those familiar with the New Testament. For all the three New Testament quotes of "Thou art my Son; this day have I begotten thee" (Acts 13:33; Heb. 1:5; Heb. 5:5) refer to the Lord Jesus Christ.

The "Son" indicates the heir apparent to the throne and "day" indicates a specific day. And "begotten" in Hebrew means "to bear or bring forth"[28], related to lineage. Alexander MacLaren considers this as the day of Jesus' resurrection:

> It is to be observed that in our psalm the day of the King's self-attestation is the day of His being "begotten". The point of time referred to is not the beginning of personal existence, but of investiture with royalty. With accurate insight, then, into the meaning of the words, the New Testament takes them as fulfilled in the Resurrection (Acts xiii. 33; Rom. 1. 4). In it, as the first step in the process which was completed in the Ascension, the manhood of Jesus was lifted above the limitations and weaknesses of the earth, and began to rise to the throne. The day of his resurrection was, as it were, the day of the birth of His humanity into royal glory.[29]

Additionally, in the New Testament, in Acts, we read about the time God enacted this. At His resurrection, Jesus was "begotten: "God hath fulfilled

---

28   Strong, s.v. "yâlad," 49.
29   MacLaren, ibid.

the same unto us their children, in that he hath raised up Jesus again, as it is also written in the second psalm, Thou art my Son; this day have I begotten[30] thee" (Acts 13:33).

His being both raised up and begotten are here mentioned in the same breath, and the next four verses continue the resurrection theme introduced in verses thirty through thirty-two. The quote then of "thou art my Son, this day have I begotten thee" comes in the middle of an eight-verse discourse on the resurrection.

On the other hand, all the "begats" in Matthew 1:2-16, plus the "conceived" of Matthew 1:20, and the "born" of Matthew 1:16, 2:1 and 4 and Luke 1:35, plus *all* the instances of "born" in John's gospel use this same Greek word, as does Galatians 4:29, where Paul writes of those "born after the Spirit". Consequently, many commentators consider "this day" to be the time when Jesus was conceived and physically born into the world as a baby, conception and birth both being indicated by the above word, which was also used in Acts 13:33. His incarnation was in God's plan from eternity (I Pet. 1:20; Rev. 13:8). Jesus was both human and Divine.

The book of Hebrews also testifies. After quoting Psalm 2:7—"Thou art my Son; this day have I begotten thee"—it reads, "When he bringeth in the firstbegotten into the world", speaking of the physical birth of Jesus and using a Greek noun[31] (Heb. 1:5, 6; cf. Luke 2:7, where it is translated "firstborn"). This word is also used of the resurrection in Colossians 1:15 and 18—"firstborn" and "firstborn from the dead"—and in Romans 8:29, "the firstborn among many brethren". Putting this all together, it appears that "firstborn", "begotten", and "firstbegotten" all indicate not only His eternal nature—the Word *with* God (John 1:1)—but also His physical conception, birth, and resurrection, plus the progression of God's resurrecting work in believers.

---

30 Strong, s.v. "gĕnnaō," 20.
31 Strong, s.v. "prōtotokos," 62.

Lastly, the Psalm 2 verse is quoted in Hebrews 5:5 as, "Thou art my Son, to day have I begotten thee", in explanation of how God glorified Jesus as the High Priest "after the order of Melchisedec" (vv. 6, 10).

So while "this day" as *one* specific day would be the normal conclusion, which of the above should we choose? Considering that some prophecies may have more than one fulfilment (Jer. 31:15, as an example), "this day have I begotten thee" seems to have at least *three* fulfilments within Jesus' lifetime. He was brought forth by God when He was conceived in Mary's womb by the Holy Spirit, then born as a baby, then begotten by being raised up after the crucifixion.

Here, then, is a summary of the three main words used:

1. *Gĕnnaō*[32] (vb.)—*to generate.* "Ye must be born again [i.e., from above]" (John 3:3, 7). In Acts 13:33, quoting Psalm 2:7, Paul uses this word for "begotten" regarding the resurrection of Jesus. First John uses it nine times—seven translated "born" and two "begotten", in reference to those conceived, gendered, or generated by God's Spirit. For example, we read in I John 5:1, 4, "Whosoever believeth that Jesus is the Christ is born of God, and every one that loveth him that begat loveth him also that is begotten of him . . . For whatsoever is born of God overcometh the world". And we also read in 1 John 5:18, "Whosoever is born of God sinneth not: but he that is begotten of God keepeth himself, and that wicked one toucheth him not". Having been born physically into the world, we now have the new birth by God's Spirit. In First Peter 1:3, "The God and Father of our Lord Jesus Christ . . . hath begotten us again unto a lively hope by the resurrection of Jesus Christ from the dead". And Paul begat spiritual progeny in this way through the Gospel (I Cor. 4:15). We should read this in conjunction with the references to physical conception and birth mentioned above. All

---

32   Strong, s.v. "gĕnnaō," 20.

three New Testament quotes of Psalm 2:7 use this word. It indicates a kind of "genetic" similarity (see three below).

2. *Prōtotokos*[33]—(adj.) *the foremost produced*: (Heb.1:6; Rev. 1:5; Rom. 8:29; Col. 1:15, 18). This can speak of the physical birth of Christ (Heb. 1:5, 6; Luke 2:7) *and* of His being the "firstborn from the dead" or "the first begotten of the dead" (Col.1:18; Rev. 1:5)—the archetype or prototype of the "church of the firstborn [i.e., born-again believers who will be physically resurrected in the future]" (Heb. 12:23). This latter verse is a parallel to the first point, relating to the resurrection of Jesus, as with all the other biblical references, including, "whom God hath raised up, having loosed the pains of death" (Acts 2:24) and "whom God raised from the dead" (Acts 4:10).

3. *Mŏnŏgĕnēs*[34]—(adj.) *"genetically" identical*. Apart from Hebrews 11:17 regarding Abraham's second but especially beloved son, Isaac, there are five occurrences in John's writings (four in his gospel and one in the first epistle of John) referring to Jesus' advent and work of redemption: "the only begotten of the Father" (John 1:14) and the "only begotten Son" (John 1:18; 3:16, 18; I John 4:9). Hence, the Son is monogenous—in a sense, "genetically" identical to His Father—as expressed in "I and my Father are one" (John 10:30).

Regarding, "Ask of me, and I shall give thee the heathen for thine inheritance, and the uttermost parts of the earth for thy possession" (v. 8), Maclaren states, "Built upon this exaltation to royalty and sonship follows the promise of universal dominion."[35]

The couplet following "ask of me" connects the nouns "heathen" and "inheritance" with "uttermost parts" and "possession". Jesus further quotes from His Father, and what God says to Him is significant because God here

---

33   Strong, s.v. "prōtotokos," 62.
34   Strong, s.v. "mŏnŏgĕnēs," 49.
35   MacLaren, ibid.

invites Him to deliberately *ask* of God for an heirloom and a possession. The couplet is synthetical parallelism—the phrases almost identical, albeit with people as the focus of the first, and land, seemingly, of the second.

The wider application is reiterated throughout the Bible, as in Daniel 7:13, 14: "And there was given him dominion, and glory, and a kingdom, that all people, nations, and languages, should serve him" (v. 14a). The request is echoed in Jesus' prayer asking God "for them also which shall believe on me through their word, that they all may be one" (John 17:20, 21). This is His "inheritance in the saints" (Eph. 1:18).

His instructions to His disciples further reflect how this was to take place: "Ye shall be witnesses unto me . . . unto the uttermost part of the earth" (Acts 1:8). God gives, in the sense of bestowing the nations as an inheritance[36] and the *whole* estate, even to the farthest extremities, for His Son's possession after His resurrection: "All power is given unto me in heaven and in earth" (Matt. 28:18).

What follows in Psalm 2 gives little hint of an exclusively pastoral context. For "thou shalt break them with a rod of iron; thou shalt dash them in pieces like a potter's vessel" could only partially be applied to Jesus' chastening of His people to develop their devotion to Him, as we read of in Hebrews 12. Instead, its direct applicability to the breaking of the nations who oppose His truth and reign is a reminder of Daniel's prophecy about the Stone cut out without hands, which broke to pieces the image (Dan. 2:34; Matt. 21:42-44). The concept is found throughout Scripture, and we will delve into it further in Psalm 91:8.[37] Several other pertinent references will suffice here. For example, while He judges the poor and advocates for the meek, He also will "smite the earth with the rod of his mouth, and with the breath of his lips shall he slay the wicked" (Isa. 11:4, this being clearly a passage referring, from its first verse, to Jesus as the One coming forth as a Rod out of Jesse's stem and a Branch out of Jesse's roots).

---

36 God gives to His people "the heritage of the heathen" (Psalm 111:6).
37 God's words to Jeremiah, for example, are like the Psalm 2 statement (Jer. 1:10, 11).

"Rod" is repeated in another Messianic psalm—"the sceptre of thy kingdom is a right sceptre" (Psalm 45:6), quoted in Hebrews 1:8 as "a sceptre of righteousness". This rod could be for fighting, punishing, walking, or writing, hence also a symbol of royal rule, not only for punishment but also for comfort (i.e., Psalm 23:4 says, "Thy rod and thy staff they comfort me"; and Micah 7:14 says, "Feed[38] thy people with thy rod, the flock of thine heritage"). The rod or sceptre is not only from Jesus; the tribe of Judah is also described as "the sceptre" (Gen. 49:10; Num. 24:17), Israel as "the rod of his inheritance" (Jer. 10:16), and the one who overcomes and keeps Jesus' works to the end as one who will "rule with a rod of iron" (Rev. 2:27, quoting from Psalm 2:9— including the second half: "as the vessels of a potter shall they be broken to shivers" with Jesus adding, "even as I received of my Father"). Clearly then, some will participate in the Son of God's reign.

The final word is from the One Who will rule: "And she[39] brought forth a man child, who was to rule all nations with a rod of iron . . . out of his mouth goeth a sharp sword, that with it he should smite the nations: and he shall rule them with a rod of iron" (Rev. 12:5a; 19:15a). This completes the New Testament quotations of Psalm 2, including those of verse seven. It is highly significant that the three New Testament references to this verse nine are all in the book of Revelation (2:27; 12:5; 19:15), the first referring to "he that overcometh", and the second and third to the One who will "rule them with a rod of iron".

In the face of all this, we should note that the word "rule" in all three of these latter references is "to tend" like a shepherd (see above regarding Micah 7:14: "Feed thy people with thy rod"). Matthew 2:6 speaks of the "Governor, that shall rule my people Israel" (see Isa. 40:11). And this use of "feed" is in John 21:16, Acts 20:28, and Revelation 7:17. Again, the pastoral touch is there, even for those who require the firmer hand.

---

38 Strong, s.v. "râ'âh," 109.
39 I.e., "the woman"—Israel.

Nevertheless, the qualifying phrase "with a rod of iron" remains, and the poetic imagery of a pot being dashed to pieces confirms the impact of the ultimate Governor, in league with His people, ruling from Heaven and establishing God's kingdom on earth—breaking down first, and then building up (Eccl. 3:3).

How that takes place is anticipated in the New Testament. For example, in Revelation 11:18, we see that though the nations will get angry, God's "wrath" also comes to judge; for while rewarding His servants, the prophets and saints and those who fear His name, both small and great, He also will destroy those who destroy the earth. Refer also to Psalm 91 and two other Messianic psalms: 21:8-13 and 24:7-10, the "King of glory . . . the LORD strong and mighty, the LORD mighty in battle" of Psalm 24 being the same "King/ Son" as that of Psalm 2.

ORDERS, WARNINGS, BLESSING

STROPHE FOUR

"Be wise now therefore, O ye kings: be instructed, ye judges of the earth. Serve the Lord with fear, and rejoice with trembling. Kiss the Son, lest he be angry, and ye perish from the way, when his wrath is kindled but a little. Blessed are all they that put their trust in him." (vv. 10-12)

STROPHE FOUR BEGINS WITH God's instructions to both those who "set themselves" and "take counsel together" against Him as well as others who are kings or judges; that is, people involved in passing legal judgments or sentences or otherwise engaged in litigation, vindication, or punishment, or anyone in law or local or international political affairs.

So much of Psalms 2 and 91 is readily relatable to current events, as well as to events throughout history and into the future. To relate them would involve endless examples and applications. Rather, what is written here is designed to help encourage you to apply the Word of God immediately to life and life's contexts. Tomorrow, in a year, a decade, and beyond, multiple situations will arise in which to apply these same scriptures. "The word of the Lord endureth forever" (I Peter 1:25).

That said, a note needs to be made about the nature of many rulers today. Without doubt, control and domination has characterised much of the world's leadership. In Luke 4:6, Satan boasted that all the power and the glory of the kingdoms of this world were his: "All this power will I give thee, and the glory of them: for that is delivered unto me; and to whomsoever I will I give it." He then offered that same power to Jesus if He would just fall down in front of him and worship him. Jesus did not dispute Satan's claim but rather focused on the worship issue, rebuking Satan and affirming that God was the only One to be worshipped. He confirmed later that Satan was the "prince" of this world" (John 12:31; 14:30; 16:11; Eph. 2:2).

In his bragging, however, Satan could have been overstating his authority, since Paul the Apostle remarked that good rulers "are not a terror to good works, but to the evil" (Rom. 13:3), and such powers were ordained by God and could not exist without Him (v. 1). The context was clearly of those who rule well and not the other way around; indeed, such rulers must have existed in Paul's time for him to say that. Today, we would call them—and still many exist— "God-fearers". But to state that a Stalin or a Pol Pot was ordained of God would be completely out of context with what Paul said, for such rulers, obviously *allowed* to exist by God but in biblical times only in a sense "ordained" by Him for purposes of judgement upon His people, are not *sanctioned* by God; they are the rulers who seize and retain control by evil spiritual powers, which in turn rule them ("the rulers of the darkness of this world", Eph. 6:12).

And Jesus will ultimately "put down all rule and all authority and power" (i.e., world rulers both spiritual and physical). And His enemies will be put under His feet (I Cor. 15:24, 25). In the New Testament, the word for normal local rulers was *pŏlitarchēs*,[40] as in Acts 17:6 and 8, or *hēgĕmōn*,[41] as in Mark 13:9.

Job argued that "the earth is given into the hand of the wicked" (Job 9:24). But variations and levels of power can be exercised by good or bad leaders. While a president or prime minister who listens to lies will end up with a government full of evil people (Prov. 29:12), one of understanding and

---

40   Strong, s.v. "pŏlitarchēs," 59.
41   Strong, s.v. "hēgĕmōn," 35.

knowledge will benefit the state (Prov. 28:2). Proverbs 29:2 declares, "When the righteous are in authority, the people rejoice: but when the wicked beareth rule, the people mourn." You will be able to apply all this quite appropriately to whatever political situation you are currently in!

God's message, though—throughout the ages, now, and in the future—is the same, namely that rulers should be wise, and "judges" should be willing to be instructed (which includes allowing themselves to be corrected) by God. In practical terms and by way of example, the thread of early English common law illustrated how this might play out, with all its struggles to retain God's laws; for the common law was linked with the natural law and derived from the Divine law—in other words, common law's origin was God. His varying imprints on culture boil down to this: God's ways and laws are *over* and *above* anything invented *outside* of His influence. And perhaps an appropriate message to all in politics and law, indeed to everyone, is contained in the memorable words of Proverbs 4:5-12, of which verse seven is pivotal: "Wisdom is the principal thing; therefore get wisdom: and with all thy getting get understanding."

This, again, must translate into action. "Serve the Lord with fear, and rejoice with trembling" (v. 11). This fear refers here to awe, affection, reverence, and respect for God and His laws. Everything we do that is right and good can be in service to Him, with rejoicing. The awe is there, though, because God is not a convenience to cater to our sinful whims and proclivities. In fact, since this psalm is directed particularly at rulers ("kings"), our God is One who looks at the way His earth—His creation—is "defiled under the inhabitants thereof; because they have transgressed the laws, changed the ordinance, broken the everlasting covenant. Therefore hath the curse devoured the earth, and they that dwell therein are desolate" (Isa. 24:5, 6). And God will "punish . . . the kings of the earth upon the earth" (v. 21). Therefore, only one other option is before them if they wish to escape that judgement, and that is to repent and choose to serve God, who revealed His love for His creation from the beginning.

The couplet is mostly synthetical: "serve" equates with "rejoice"; "fear" matches with "trembling". While rejoicing and trembling might sound contradictory, once the holiness of God is appreciated, the paradox makes sense: serve and rejoice with reverence and trembling respect for this mighty God of the universe, Whose names we will explore more in Psalm 91. The service we give is our lives and, likewise, for kings, judges, and politicians. "Ye that love the LORD, hate evil" (Psalm 97:10).

The penultimate sentence of Psalm 2 is challenging: "Kiss the Son, lest he be angry, and ye perish from the way, when his wrath is kindled but a little". (v. 12) "Kiss" is not only what it seems at face value. Of course, as a greeting in many places in the world, including the Middle East, the kiss at least indicates friendliness. "Thou gavest me no kiss" (Luke 7:45). "Greet one another with an holy kiss" (II Cor. 13:12; I Thess. 5:26; I Pet. 5:14)[42]. This word is intensified in the following cases, where the kissing is more passionate:

- Luke 7:38—the woman who anointed Jesus' feet "kissed his feet";
- Luke 15:20—the father's response to seeing his prodigal son return was that he "fell on his neck and kissed him";
- Acts 20:37—the elders of the church at Ephesus "fell on Paul's neck and kissed him".

"Kiss the Son", then, means to be friendly towards, to connect with, to love and delight in. "Kiss" here is normally used for the physical act of kissing, but also metaphorically, as in Psalm 85:10, "righteousness and peace have kissed each other".

An often-used word in the New Testament for "worship" means to "make obeisance, do reverence to"[43] with the sense of prostration and kissing *towards*

---

42   Strong, s.v. "philŏs," 76.
43   W.E. Vine, *An Expository Dictionary of New Testament Words*, s.v. "proskuneō" (Iowa Falls: Riverside Book and Bible House, 1952) 1247.

something or someone. It implies rendering respect to someone and links in with the earlier meaning of "kiss the Son".

So to the kings and the judges, God says that they should serve Him, rejoice in Him, love Him, delight in His ways, and reverence His Son—all the opposite of what many had, have been, and are doing. In other words, they must repent and convert to follow God.

Interestingly, the text here borrows from the Chaldean for "Son"[44], still meaning the heir apparent to the throne but a different word to verse seven's Hebrew. God was speaking to those outside Israel, too! This Chaldean word is used elsewhere in the Bible in Ezra, Daniel, and Proverbs 31:2. Some, like Alexander Maclaren, believe that this text, "Kiss the Son", is uncertain in meaning, other than possibly "take hold of instruction"[45] (The Septuagint, LXX, Targum). Either way, the underlying message is similar.

Angry in "lest he be angry[46]" is also onomatopoeic, connected with breathing hard as in a rage, as if someone is saying, "Enough!" "And ye perish from the way" (see also Psalm 91:11 where the same word is used for "ways"). The very next phrase repeats the sentiment with the warning that one ought to not give occasion for God's wrath to be kindled. Wrath comes from the same word for "angry". But we are reminded by "but a little" that this anger only needs to be mild—relative to its potential full force that is—for it to be effective. Perhaps this will help keep it in perspective for us for we may think "anger" is only reserved for humans or petulant heathen gods or goddesses and not the Creator Who revealed Himself as love. We will be investigating a similar theme in our Psalm 91 study. Remember that at one time, while on earth, Jesus "looked round about on them with anger" (Mark 3:5). The anger described in Psalm 2 is the natural reaction of God seeing His people and His earth devastated. And the rulers' responses can be of indifference, hostility, or a willingness to obey God.

---

44 Strong, s.v. "bar," 23.
45 MacLaren, ibid.
46 Strong, s.v. "'ânaph," 15.

Finally, as Psalm 1 begins with a beatitude and as Psalm 91 finishes with eight blessings in its last three verses, so Psalm 2 ends with a beatitude: "Blessed are all they that put their trust in him." (v. 12b). The benedictive beatitudes in Psalms 1 and 2 are like double bookends—a superscription and a subscription—in what is essentially a double-psalmed introduction to the psalter. Both use the word "blessed".

Putting one's trust in God is a decision. The result, indeed, is blessing, as we will find out later in Psalm 91:4, where we also find this word, "trust".

Psalm 2 is a message to kings, rulers, and judges, but also to all those who "put their trust in him"—"him" in its last verse being the "Son", the Lord Jesus Christ, Who we shall meet again in the final word of the final verse of Psalm 91.

PART TWO
PSALM 91

THE PLACE OF TRUST UNDER
THE SHADOW OF GOD

STROPHE ONE

He that dwelleth in the secret place of the most High shall abide under the shadow of the Almighty.[47] (v. 1)

STROPHE TWO

I will say of the LORD, He is my refuge and my fortress: my God; in him will I trust. (v. 2)

STROPHE THREE

Surely he shall deliver thee from the snare of the fowler, and from the noisome pestilence.

He shall cover thee with his feathers, and under his wings shalt thou trust: his truth shall be thy shield and buckler.

Thou shalt not be afraid for the terror by night; nor for the arrow that flieth by day;

Nor for the pestilence that walketh in darkness; nor for the destruction that wasteth at noonday.

---

47   The *antithesis* of Strophe One of Psalm 2

A thousand shall fall at thy side, and ten thousand at thy right hand; but it shall not come nigh thee.

Only with thine eyes shalt thou behold and see the reward of the wicked.

Because thou hast made the LORD, which is my refuge, even the most High, thy habitation;

There shall no evil befall thee, neither shall any plague come nigh thy dwelling.

For he shall give his angels charge over thee, to keep thee in all thy ways.

They shall bear thee up in their hands, lest thou dash thy foot against a stone.

Thou shalt tread upon the lion and adder: the young lion and the dragon shalt thou trample under feet. (vv. 3-13)

STROPHE FOUR

Because he hath set his love upon me, therefore will I deliver him: I will set him on high, because he hath known my name.

He shall call upon me, and I will answer him: I will be with him in trouble; I will deliver him, and honour him.

With long life will I satisfy him, and shew him my salvation. (vv. 14-16)

CHAPTER 1

INTRODUCTION TO PSALM 91

PSALM 91 IS SUPERB literature. While at first glance, it seems to speak of unreachable ideals, to argue that its promises are implausible or impossible is to deny its Divine inspiration, the dismissal of which ends either in ignorance or in cherry-picking preferred passages. In contrast, some see it as fool-proof insurance against any and every trial or minor ailment. As fallen creatures, we have indeed acquired an astonishing capacity for muddle! The Word of God, however, nowhere encourages presumptuous thinking or assumptions of protection from rash, unwise, or uninformed decisions.

The purpose of the Scriptures in informing and encouraging our faith is to motivate us to aspire to get more right in every area of life. For example, while our bodies are equipped by God with amazing repair and renewal mechanisms, the fallen world presents to us significant challenges. Regardless of exercise, vegetables, vitamins, medical advice, or wise decisions, those mechanisms are continually being tested. Most of the time, the hazards are successfully battled without our awareness; but the fallen world surrounds us, with many threats sadly also being manmade.

Does Psalm 91 speak into any of this? Does it speak into how our physical, psychological, emotional, and spiritual lives can come under God's preserving, even healing influence? The answer is that in many ways—perhaps more than we may have thought—it does.

We read about Moses, for instance, who got to the end of his life with undiminished stamina. Is that possible? For us? Even a little? And how could we ever find out unless we were to take passages such as Psalm 91 seriously? We are instructed to have Scripture residing in our hearts and minds as "daily bread", from whence comes the sustenance of its promises, encouragements, and challenges.

Psalm 91 is a majestic psalm because it encompasses all that is relevant to the believer's faith and because of its rich, powerful language, its figures of speech, its revelation of God's majesty, and its promises of what God will do for those who set their love upon Him and put their trust in Him. It covers every aspect of our lives and describes where all humans, in theory, could be. And the only way to know if it "works" is to take it seriously. This study is designed to help you do that.

The psalm's structure is set up in this fashion:

- Strophe One—verse one
- Strophe Two—verse two
- Strophe Three—verses three to thirteen
- Strophe Four—verses fourteen to sixteen

Characteristic of the psalm is to change subject pronouns between strophes. The first strophe introduces the theme of the psalm. The second is the speaker's simple statement of faith. The third is an address to a fellow truster in God. The fourth is God's speaking to the one trusting. For convenience, I have divided the longest strophe (Strophe Three) into five chapters.

The psalm has no name to it. Some say Moses authored it. If so, along with Psalm 90 and probably Psalm 92, it would constitute the earliest of the Psalms chronologically. Psalm 91 seems to relate to Moses' experience: lions and serpents, miracles of deliverance, as in the exodus from Egypt with the Israelites spared from the plagues and pestilences around them, his personal closeness to God, the "arrow" and the "terror", his experience of protection from various threats, his long life—all point to Moses as a potential candidate for authorship. However, this is not conclusive, since David (who the Septuagint suggests is the author) also witnessed miraculous deliverances and used similar language—sometimes with identical phrases—in his psalms. Psalm 57 is an example.

The fact that we cannot ascertain exactly who the author of Psalm 91 is benefits us in one sense because it provides an extra sense of mystery. And certainty about who the author was might colour our thinking, especially knowing that David and Moses, though with great strengths, also had significant weaknesses. Authorial anonymity further protects us from the error of dismissing it as being only from the days of Moses or David, an error that might tempt us to consider it irrelevant or inapplicable today. What does show up here though is that authorship of the Psalms is by no means a simple and straightforward matter. "In most cases . . . the quest for an individual author is pointless. The making of the Hebrew Bible is owed to the scribal class rather than a limited number of individuals. We should not be looking for authors but seeking to penetrate the mind-set of the scribal elite".[48]

A possibility is that Psalm 91 could be primarily Messianic. An extensive understanding of the Trinity could assist a hypothesis of the whole psalm being so, and shed light on the matter of the speakers. Satan identified it with Jesus in the gospels as he tried to tempt Him. But how may a Messianic psalm be defined? Is it one in which the Messiah speaks throughout or only occasionally? Or is it one that speaks *about* the Messiah, where God speaks of Him, as in Psalm 2? Psalms such as Psalm 24 and Psalm 45 clearly point to the Messiah, and other psalms also have prophecies of Him. But if the Messiah is speaking in Psalm 91, can it be applied to us, too? Or should none be applied to us or to the readers of the psalmist's day but *only* to the Messiah, in which

---

48   Karel Van Der Toorn, *Scribal Culture and the Making of the Hebrew Bible* (Cambridge, Massachusetts: Harvard University Press, 2007), 5.

case "he", "I", and "thee" should solely be in reference to the Messiah and to no one else?

With the probability of an Old Testament audience having a limited understanding of the Trinity, one would expect this psalm to have been initially aimed at *them* rather than being solely Messianic, regardless of the fact that a perfect fulfilment of it would naturally be applicable to Jesus and the psalm would have been close to His heart. Jesus' temptation after forty days in the wilderness when He was "with the wild beasts", and the fact that "the angels ministered unto him" (Mark 1:13), remind us of verses eleven, twelve, and thirteen. In Matthew and Luke, we read of how Satan used Psalm 91's verses eleven and twelve to try to tempt Jesus. But was he using these verses because he thought that the *whole* psalm applied solely or, at least, primarily to Jesus? If so, the problematic parts would be where Jesus, as God in the flesh, apparently speaks to "the LORD" in verses one and two and decides to trust in God. (The reference in the Messianic Psalm 110, a companion to Psalm 2, that reads "the LORD said unto my Lord" is clearly to be comprehended from a trinitarian viewpoint.)

Was Satan putting the whole psalm to the test by misquoting verses eleven and twelve? We do not have sufficient proof of this, but neither do we have a way of proving it not to be true. For example, Jesus will surely "see the reward of the wicked", maybe even being the cause of it, and no evil could befall Him since He unquestionably could triumphantly "trample" upon those lions, adders, young lions, and dragons. The "seed of the woman" (Jesus) would "bruise", or overwhelm, the serpent's (Satan's) head (Gen. 3:15) (i.e., Jesus was destined to overwhelm Satan's work through both His earthly ministry and His sacrifice for the world's sins—Heb. 2:14; I John 3:8). Jesus' being "bruised" in the "heel" was Satan's seemingly short-lived "victory" at Calvary. The "seed of the woman" is also those followers of Jesus who would "bruise" Satan's head, while he, in turn, would "bruise" their heel, in the intense struggle of the ages. And God Himself would "bruise" (i.e., crush[49]) Satan under their feet (Rom. 16:20).

---

49   Strong, s.v. "suntribō," 69.

You can see the application widening up already, and it does not make sense that God would have allowed people at the time of its writing to assume the psalm to be irrelevant to themselves as believers in God. Anyone reading it the first time would have easily considered it personally relevant.

So although it may also be referring to the Messiah, the main message of Psalm 91 is to the believer; and this study will focus on that message in its dramatic narrations. Jesus in His incarnation would have been familiar with *all* the Psalms, with many featuring in His prayers and teachings. He quoted from them. But making Psalm 91 exclusively Messianic further ignores the fact that it opens with what strongly sounds like an invitation to *us*, drawing us to the possibility that *any* reader who takes it seriously can also dwell "in the secret place of the most High" and "abide under the shadow of the Almighty".

To clear up one point about the speakers in the psalm, the idea has been suggested that pronouns such as "I", "me", "my", "he", "him", "thee", "thy", and "thou" in the Psalms can also mean "we", referring to a kind of corporate personality. Thus (so goes the theory) a psalm could be about an individual *and* a nation. This is an implausibility in most cases (though not all) and hence this study primarily points to personal rather than national application.

The issue of who is speaking where in the psalm, however, is somewhat more complex than it is in Psalm 2. Since a few scenarios present themselves, I will give some possibilities. Whichever way, the strophes remain the same. Remember, we are thinking of the speakers, not the author, for the author was most likely only one. The speakers then (or we could use the term *voices*), could be one, two, or three.

First, one speaker is seen throughout, addressing the believer in verse one, himself in the next verse, then someone or anyone through to verse thirteen, including a brief phrase again about himself in verse nine, and finally quoting God directly in the last three verses.

Second, two speakers are seen, with the first relating all the psalm up until God speaks in verses fourteen to sixteen. Alternatively, God could be speaking throughout the psalm, except verse two, plus the interpolation in verse nine.

Third, three speakers or voices are seen. We could think of it as the song it is. Even more, we could imagine it as an oratorio: the first and main voice (or choir) in verse one giving the introductory theme about the dweller in the secret place of the most High lodging under the shadow of the Almighty. Here, in this curtain-raiser, all stops could be pulled out as it announces its overarching statement of profound and universal spiritual truths, perhaps sung in fortissimo or alternatively pianissimo with the onomatopoeic /ʃ/—"sh" sounds of "shall", "shadow", and adding in the Hebrew for the Almighty[50], all illustrating the place of quiet holiness.

The second voice (a solo?) then enters with a personal declaration of faith in verse two—another fortissimo, perhaps—exclaiming, "I will say of the LORD", followed by a proclamation to himself or anyone listening that God is his refuge and fortress, the One in whom he trusts. The first voice begins the next section with "Surely", a Handelian chorus maybe, laying forth the blessings and benefits resulting from speaker two's emphatic statement of faith briefly repeated in the verse nine interjection (though some argue that the translation there should be "thy refuge").

Finally, the voice of God enters with His blessing of speaker two.

Fourth—and back to two voices: all the psalm, except verse two as God's voice—verse one being about Jesus, verse two relating Jesus' personal statement, verses three to thirteen God's speaking *to* Jesus, and verses fourteen to sixteen being God's narrative about His favour and blessing on Jesus. But that would make it Messianic.

The option which appears to me to be the most plausible is the second—two speakers: one from verses one to thirteen, and then the second, God, from verses fourteen to sixteen.

---

50   Strong, s.v. "Shadday," 113.

Five times, Psalm 91 speaks of its main theme, the place of the believer, the blessed one who:

1. Dwells in God's secret place,
2. Lives under God's shadow,
3. Has God as his refuge,
4. Has God as his fortress,
5. Has God as his habitation.

"Deliver" occurs three times, each time with a different Hebrew word, the believer being:

1. Delivered from snares and plagues,
2. Delivered and helped (set on high),
3. Delivered and honoured.

"Pestilence" is mentioned twice and "plague" once:

1. The worrying pestilence,
2. The concealed pestilence,
3. The plague.

Four threats ought not to be feared; two things angels can do; twelve things God does; and twelve the believer does.

If we do not see a passage of Scripture in its proper context, it could lead to a wrong interpretation. Some may even consider God's Word as not being for today and, hence, dismiss it as irrelevant and out-of-date, although perhaps respecting its literary value. Those of a liberal theological persuasion or who are agnostic may dismiss certain sections. And others may say that though true, it all relates to a different era, or that while it may apply today, there is no cast-iron certainty. Thus, they may question how fool-proof it is, or whether disappointment and doubt about God's goodness might result if people fail to get what they want from it.

Hyper-faith may well lead some to take liberties in their reading of it, ultimately resulting—for them—in judgmentalism, self-condemnation, and confusion. At another extreme, a few might say that it works for only those of their particular persuasion; or for only those born again; or for only those born again and baptised in the Spirit; or for those born again, baptised in the Spirit, and who speak in tongues; or for only those who can recite it all by heart!

But Christianity is not a checklist of rules. We sometimes like to think that if only we could keep *all* the rules, then life would work better. In many instances, that is true; for example, keeping the rules of the road, while no absolute guarantee, will undoubtedly help the journey go better and safer than not keeping them. In finding God, though, the Bible states that it does not work that way. Rather, any "checklist" is to be one of principles applied by faith. Spiritual outcomes cannot be generated by what we *do* only but by what we believe and then apply.

Our focus is to be more on the process than the outcome, the relationship more than the blessings. Jesus said, "Seek ye first the kingdom of God, and his righteousness; and all these things [food, drink, clothing—and by extension our needs on every level] shall be added unto you" (Matt. 6:33). Why it might "work" for some but not for others would not immediately be related to the psalm but to the way all of Scripture is being approached.

With a sound theology, it is entirely legitimate to take Psalm 91 as an expression of eternal and Divine truth. To approach it any other way can easily lead to cherry-picking whichever passages one prefers. On the other hand, wise exegesis compares Scripture with Scripture. And if a promise is manifestly absolute—that is, you do this, and such and such will happen—then what reason do we have to question it? If it does not apply all the time or on occasion only, then the problem is not with God. Life is not always going to go as we wish, but perhaps we must, in the first instance, look to ourselves for the reasons as our wishes might be coming from misguided thinking. Surely, God is the One to get the benefit of the doubt. And as students of Scripture, our call is to respond rightly to God's revelation.

Read on, as this resource will help you become more familiar with Psalm 91 and its Author.

CHAPTER 2

LIVING IN THE SECRET PLACE

STROPHE ONE

"He that dwelleth in the secret place of the most High shall abide under the shadow of the Almighty." (v. 1)

IN THE HEBREW, IT reads "in the secret of the most High" or "in the cover of the most High". Cover, secret, shelter, or hiding place comes from a verb which means to conceal by covering[51]. It is used in Psalm 17:8—"Hide me under the shadow of thy wings"—and in Psalm 64:2—"Hide me from the secret counsel of the wicked". And the noun and the verb together are in Psalm 27:5b: "In the secret of his tabernacle shall he hide me" and again in Psalm 31:20a: "Thou shalt hide them in the secret of thy presence from the pride of man".

"Shadow" is "shade" or "defence". Several other examples are:

- Psalm 17:8: "Hide me under the shadow of thy wings".
- Psalm 36:7b: "The children of men put their trust under the shadow of thy wings".
- Psalm 63:7: "In the shadow of thy wings will I rejoice".

---

51   Strong, s.v. "çâthar," 84.

The phrase "secret place" will initially mean different things to different people. Some connotations will be positive and some not. For example, people who are introverted or creative (or both), such as artists and musicians, sometimes speak of a "space"—perhaps physical, perhaps more indistinct and hard-to-define—where they can find themselves and be creative. Others such as the more philosophically minded or those who simply feel the need to do so have designated or unprompted times away from the hustle and bustle— times to contemplate and reflect. Terms such as "getting centred", "chilling out", or "getting focused" are sometimes used to describe this. We could think perhaps of a specific room or the countryside or somewhere near the sea where we can leave stress, difficult relationships, conflicts, and politics behind. Some may stay put but close off all thoughts and emotions related to what has been going on around them, and this may be helpful in some situations. Others find somewhere to pray and seek God. Most, if not all, of us have some version of the "secret place".

But there can be dark ones, too. Satan has his counterfeits. Undisclosed places lurk deep in people's hearts, forbidding others from entering. Such places harbour murky thoughts, private hatreds and grievances, and plots and schemes. Liars, thieves, fraudsters, and murderers as yet unexposed keep secret sins within their hearts, even ones that sometimes they themselves have forgotten. The result is that they live in constant denial, convinced of their innocence. And some, knowing their own sins and what they have done, have a "secret place" that is not as clandestine as they think because discerning observers can see the symptoms of their secrets.

Whether dark or not, God has tabs on it all. "For God shall bring every work into judgment, with every secret thing, whether it be good, or whether it be evil" (Eccl. 12:14). But the place spoken of in Psalm 91 is as that in Psalm 27:5: "For in the time of trouble he shall hide me in his pavilion: in the secret of his tabernacle shall he hide me; he shall set me up upon a rock" and in

Psalm 31:20: "Thou shalt hide them in the secret of thy presence from the pride of man". These passages use the same word for "secret" as does Psalm 91.

Following this first strophe is the psalm's own commentary on it. At first glance, the subject and the predicate look like a duplication of the same idea—a tautology (i.e., dwell in the secret place, and you will abide under the shadow of the Almighty; abide under the shadow of the Almighty, and you will dwell in the secret place). But the action and result—the cause and effect—is evident. You do this—here is the result; you live that way—such-and-such happens. We need to get to the secret place before we get to the shadow—the first is personal, devotional, and intimate; the second is the consequence. By dwelling in the first, we will abide in the second.

A more literal rendering might go something like this: He who settles down and sits (the same word we saw in Psalm 2:4 as "sitteth") in the hiding place of the Most High shall stay permanently under the shadow of the Supreme God (a name—"the Almighty"—that was used forty-eight times in the Old Testament, including twice in the Psalms—Psalm 68:14; 91:1—six times in Genesis, thirty-one in the poetic book of Job, and nine elsewhere).

This verse is binary in structure, both halves speaking similarly (i.e., synthetic parallelism). "Abide", however, gives the sense of permanence. Abiding under the shadow is the beginning of blessings. If you live hidden (spiritually speaking) in this secret place (unknown to those who do not know the Most High God and hence are shut out from it), then you will stay ceaselessly under the Almighty's shadow. Linked to the shadow of God—where He moves, we move. Here is guidance, as well as protection; but by extension, one could also move oneself out from under the shadow by deliberately moving out of the will of God.

Being under the shadow of the wings of a bird is an image extended in verse four. It is one of a mother. Jesus spoke of Himself as being like a hen gathering her hatchlings under her wings (Luke 13:34), further implying this aspect of God. But we also have *"His* wings", with the idea of God as a Father—a Provider and a Protector.

As suggested, "dwelleth" and "abide"[52] have different shades of meaning. We could consider them as "sit" or "settle down" for the first, as in God sitting in the heavens in Psalm 2:4, and "stop over and stay" for the second. The meanings lead from one to the other, the sitting leading to the staying. Sit in God's hiding place, and you will stay permanently close to Him; settle down in the shelter of the Supreme One, and you will remain under His presence— His shadow.

First, we get into this secret place, and then He keeps us there. Think of how you have your designated quiet time in the morning and thus come under His presence all day. And whether on the bus, in the train or the car, at the office or the construction site, at home, in church, or wherever you are, you will constantly be in the "secret place of the Most High". Then, after the busyness of the day, you can refocus again and stop in with God and find His peace.

The psalmist's imagery gives a sense of reality and continuity, indicating a twenty-four-hour, seven-day-a-week experience. As we never cease to seek Him, we never move away from His covering.

"Abide", with its sense of lying down or lodging overnight or permanently (see Lev. 19:13), is also used in the following verses:

- "The fear of the LORD tendeth to life; and he that hath it shall abide satisfied[53]; he shall not be visited with evil" (Prov. 19:23; cf. Prov. 15:31)
- "He shall lie all night" (Song. 1:13)
- "Lie all night in sackcloth, ye ministers of my God" (Joel 1:13)
- "How is the faithful city become an harlot! it was full of judgment; righteousness lodged in it; but now murderers" (Isa. 1:21)

---

52 Strong, s.v. "lîyn," 59.
53 Strong, s.v. "sâbêa'," 112.

- "How long shall thy vain thoughts lodge within thee?" (Jer. 4:14)
- "Whither thou goest, I will go; and where thou lodgest, I will lodge" (Ruth 1:16).

New Testament counterparts for "abide"[54] [55] have the same sense of staying continuously at a place, remaining, tarrying, and being permanent. Examples are Luke 9:4 and 19:5; John 5:38, 15:4, 6, 7, and 10; Acts 16:15; I John 2:24, 27, 28 and 3:15; and I Corinthians 16:6.

Psalm 91 begins by focusing on the third person singular ("He") and ends with it, too, in its comprehensive statements about he who has "set his love upon me". It is thus inviting anyone to have this covenant connection with Him.

Before dealing with how to access this secret place, let us define it. It is a place of deliverance from danger ("the snare of the fowler"), from disease ("the noisome pestilence"), and from destruction (v. 6). It is a place of trust, of spiritual comfort and safety (v. 4-6), and of God's overshadowing protection—specifically angelic, angels being believers' "bodyguards" who intervene when necessary (vv. 11-12). It is a place of triumph over both human and demonic enemies (v. 13) and thus of spiritual security ("I will set him on high"), of answered prayer ("I will answer him"), of fellowship with God ("I will be with him in trouble"), of honour ("and honour him"), satisfaction ("I will satisfy him") and salvation ("and shew him my salvation").

So, we have:

1. Deliverance
2. Divine comfort and safety
3. Protection
4. Triumph
5. Spiritual security

---

54   Strong, s.v. "měnō," 47.
55   Strong, s.v. "paraměnō," 55.

6. Answered prayer

7. Fellowship with God (especially in difficult times)

8. Honour

9. Satisfaction

10. Salvation

The word is also used in Deuteronomy 32:38, where God taunts rebellious Israel regarding the whereabouts of their false gods, saying, "Let them rise up and help you, and be your protection", and also when God reveals secrets to people (Dan. 2:22, 28).

Why is it a secret? Here is where sin and evil cannot enter and evildoers have no access. In fact, their unwillingness to avail themselves of its benefits will end up in eternal regret for them. Amongst those who understand what God is offering, some feel they are not "holy" enough to enter in. Yet this place is exactly where they can find true holiness once there. Psalm 27:5 states, "In the secret of his tabernacle shall he hide me". Tabernacle is a covering, tent, or home[56]. The double emphasis is there, like saying "in the concealment of his covering". God's tent is a tent of light. As observed in ancient Israel after the Exodus from Egypt, the tabernacle was where God's presence and light shone, although with a cloud at its door. The cloud by day was its covering and the fire by night its light (Exod. 40:38). Inside, too, was the candlestick signifying the light of God's Word. And the tabernacle itself was indicative of heaven, God's "tent". God could also take up residence with His people: "And I will set my tabernacle among you" (Lev. 26:11). Again, God is light (Dan. 2:22; John 1:9; I John 1:5; Rev. 21:23, 22:5), so this secret place has no darkness. Scripture points to it as a place of indescribable light, with all the ten benefits described above.

We enter by choosing specifically. First, we choose to respond to Jesus' declaration that we "must be born again [from above]" (John 3:3, 7).

---

56 Strong, s.v. "'ôhel," 9.

The apostle Paul stated that the life of faith was to be lived "through the power of the Holy Ghost" (Rom. 15:13), "power" here being a miraculous force. And in John 1:12, we read, "But as many as received him, to them gave he the power to become the sons of God". Power here is the ability, freedom, or right to become the children, the "sons" of God—those with the inheritance. This comes through repentance and acceptance by faith of the truth about Jesus. Once we have thus entered God's family, we have the privilege of developing a close relationship with our Creator. This does not mean that we are automatically placed onto a Heaven-bound conveyor belt with lifelong immunity from trouble—not if the Bible in its entirety is to mean anything. The eighth chapter of Romans tells us about the trials of the heroes of faith; and we see conflict, struggle, and challenge from start to finish. We do, however, have a permanent abiding place in Him Who is with us now and forever and in all situations.

Second, we choose to remain there on a daily basis. We sense His presence because He is with us and within us. We want to sense this constantly; but we are human, too, sometimes getting tired or upset and with the world banging at our door, whereby the sense of closeness escapes us. The powerful pull of the three temptations—"the lust of the flesh, and the lust of the eyes, and the pride of life"—is one factor (I John 2:16). These translate to excessive longings to indulge, to possess, and to impress.[57] In the original text, "lust" denotes the imposition of passion and an unnatural longing for and coveting after what is forbidden. Giving in to it swiftly swings us out of the secret place; but by turning from temptation, resisting the lures, avoiding them and praying, we can sense His presence again.

David wrote: "Be thou my strong habitation, whereunto I may continually resort" (Psalm 71:3). "Habitation" here we will see again in verse nine of Psalm 91—an abode of God, humans, or animals, a place of shelter[58]. This includes

---

57   *Studies in Christian Living, Book 5: Foundations for Faith* (Christchurch: The Navigators, 1964), 21.
58   Strong, s.v. "mâ'ôwn," 69.

the tabernacle or the temple of ancient Israel as God's abode; but clearly, David does not mean that in Psalm 71, for this is where he goes when he is in trouble ("cause me to escape . . . save me" v. 2), *not a physical but a spiritual place*, and a first, not a last, resort. So how did David go there? How did Abraham or Joseph or Moses or any godly man or woman before Jesus go there? The answer is that they went there the same way we go: in faith and by a threefold means, which will be examined in more detail below.

In the New Testament, "access" is a key word. You must have a key to access a lock, a ticket to get into an event; and the Greek word in the following verses means exactly that—admission.

- "By whom also we have access by faith into this grace wherein we stand." (Rom. 5:2)
- "For through him we both have access by one Spirit unto the Father." (Eph. 2:18; and see verse 8)
- "In whom we have boldness and access with confidence by the faith of him." (Eph. 3:12)

If sin has caused loss of connection, then confession, repentance, and faith are the keys to regain contact. The means for this is the trinity of prophecy, priest, and prayer. By prophecy, I refer to the written manuscripts which became Scripture from thousands of years ago, starting with Adam to whom "God said" and then others also spoken to by God, written down by various people and collated by Moses in Genesis, which, along with his other four books, make up the Pentateuch. Moses was a prophet (Deut. 18:15, 18—"like unto me"), a "model prophet" according to Van der Toorne.[59] The word was *nâbâ'*—to prophesy, speak, sing by inspiration. Jesus spoke in Matthew 23:2 of those who "sit in Moses' seat" (i.e., teachers of the Torah). Moses the prophet declared the Law (Deut. 1:5), which included proclaiming, expounding, and

---

59   Van der Toorne, 2007, 158.

explaining. The Israelites were likewise to teach their children (Deut. 4:10). "Prophecy", then, also includes the books of history, Psalms, Proverbs, and the major and minor prophets—all making up the Old Testament—plus the Gospels, the epistles, and the book of Revelation making up the New Testament. All is revelation.

We then see how the priests helped to regain contact. Genesis shows us how Abraham performed some priestly duties; and there was also, at that time, a high priest of God named Melchizedek. Additionally, the tribe of Levi was later set apart as priests. Moses under God's guidance set up this system with a high priest who made daily and yearly sacrifices for the sins of the people (Heb. 7:27; 9:7). Many offerings had to be made to God. The forty verses of chapter twenty-nine of the book of Numbers chronicle these, mentioning the word "offering" or "offer" seventy times! We may be thankful that we do not have to do any of that now. They did not have a High Priest in the heavenly places (Heb. 4:14) but rather a human priest, a disadvantage today for all kinds of practical reasons, not the least of which would be its laboriousness and its exclusivity. The holy of holies (the inner sanctum of the tabernacle and figurative of the secret place) was able to be accessed by that high priest only once a year.

Jesus came, however, to make a way for us to enter this secret place. And here is the point: we would have no high priest to intercede for us, to atone for our sins, or to make sacrifice for our wrongdoing were it not for one man—the perfect and sinless God-man Jesus Christ, Who made that sacrifice two thousand years ago. Paul stated, "For if that first covenant had been faultless, then should no place have been sought for the second" (Heb. 8:7). Then he re-emphasised the greatness of the New Covenant, as prophesied in the Old: "This is the covenant that I will make with them after those days, saith the Lord, I will put my laws into their hearts, and in their minds will I write them; and their sins and iniquities will I remember no more" (Heb. 10:16-17). Now we enter in, through the new birth, through the power of the

Spirit, through the sacrifice of the blood of Jesus made once for His people, and for all time (Heb. 9:12, 26-28; 10:10, 12).

"The very one who earlier had said to Christ **'Thou art my Son'** (Psalm 2:7, cf. Heb. 1:5) now has said to Him **'Thou art a priest for ever, after the order of Mechizedek'** (Psalm 110:4)."[60]

The third way we can regain connection is through prayer. Paul wrote that we need to "come boldly unto the throne of grace, that we may obtain mercy, and find grace to help in time of need" (Heb. 4:16). Being made capable of connecting with God by His Spirit within us, we must still make the choice to enter the path by prayer. His mercy ensuing from His throne of grace points us to this access by the written Word of God and our great High Priest, Jesus. Paul said, "in time of need", so when we find ourselves suddenly or unexpectedly in such seasons, or realise our inherent *constant* need, then we can respond to this call to dwell in the secret place unceasingly. Here is where we live in His grace day by day. Jesus stated that while we are born from above, those who choose to follow Him should also "strive to enter in at the strait gate" (Luke 13:24). This striving[61] happens particularly at the start of our journey. According to Jamieson, Fausset, and Brown, "The word signifies to 'contend' as for the mastery, to 'struggle,' expressive of the *difficulty* of being saved, as if one would have to *force his way in*."[62] Paul wrote that believers should "labour to enter into that rest". This matter is one of abiding (John 15:4-7; I John 2:28), by faith keeping our heart clean (I John 1:9), and our mind on Him: "Thou wilt keep him in perfect peace, whose mind is stayed on thee: because he trusteth in thee" (Isa. 26:3).

Practically, when we accept the Lord Jesus Christ, we are immediately created anew as part of God's family of believers, after which we have access

---

60   G. C. D. Howley, *A New Testament Commentary* (London: Pickering & Inglis Ltd, 1969), 548.
61   "Strong's G75 – agōnizomai," Blue Letter Bible, Accessed 21 December, 2023, https://www.blueletterbible.org/lexicon/g75/mgnt/tr/0-1/.
62   Robert Jamieson, A. R. Fausset, and David Brown, *Commentary Critical and Explanatory on the Whole Bible, vol. 2* (Oak Harbor, WA: Logos Research Systems, Inc., 1997), 113.

to all the blessings of being in His kingdom, including the fruit of and the gifts of His Spirit. But to remain consistently in this place takes effort, "labour"—not as in works of righteousness but as in a commitment to cultivating a relationship as one would with a friend or relative. That takes at least some effort. It does not happen automatically.

And the entryway can also be lonely. It may not mean that you must separate yourself completely from family, friends, and fellowship. But you *will* need to find a place of solitude, stillness, peace, prayer, praise, repentance, and confession, where you might sit, stand, kneel, walk around, whisper, worship, cry, and call upon God, seeking Him, reading and considering His Word. It will sometimes be a place of tears, even of desperation at times, having no time limit, no minimum or maximum period, but enough time—*quality* time—to allow you to become settled and centered in Him.

Most often, we need just such a daily quiet time at a private location into which others do not intrude. There we can come into that spiritual rest, that perpetual sabbath where we "lie down in green pastures" (Psalm 23:2). We have wars to win and races to run, plus struggles and tests; yet "in returning and rest" and "in quietness and in confidence", we find strength (Isa. 30:15). This is where we can be "more than conquerors through him that loved us" (Rom. 8:37).

The human soul longs for rest from strife and struggle; and at the time of our salvation, we initially receive a measure of that, being placed safely in Jesus' arms. All we need do, then, is live a Christian life pleasing to God. While accepted by God and empowered to live joyfully and contentedly, however, life's issues still require extra growth in grace—hence the need to settle regularly in that secret place and stay under the shadow of God amidst all our ups and downs. Faith works to move us forward into places where God can use us for His kingdom.

When Paul stated that "they to whom [the gospel] was first preached entered not in because of unbelief" (Heb. 4:6), he was taking the example of the children of Israel not entering the Promised Land because of their unbelief and thus illustrating an important concept about the Christian life. Here lies the answer to the mystery as to why the fourth commandment about keeping the Sabbath is the only commandment *not* specifically repeated in the New Testament, as I have touched on in my study guide on the Beatitudes. Though it still naturally holds validity in the principle of a day of physical rest, the book of Hebrews speaks of a type of rest which, paradoxically, you must *labour* to enter. As Hebrews 4:11 states, "Let us labour therefore to enter into that rest, lest any man fall after the same example of unbelief".

Here is pictured, in the Greek words, a spiritual—rather than a physical—sabbath. Several words are used for "rest" in the book of Hebrews, *except* in Hebrews 4:9, where the author coins a word[63] derived clearly from the original word for the Sabbath. This is in reference to the repose a Christian has in Christ, of which Paul also states, "There remaineth therefore a rest to the people of God".

"In time, there are many Sabbaths, but then there shall be the enjoyment and keeping of a Sabbath-rest: one perfect and eternal . . . the 'rest' in this Hebrews 4:9 is the nobler and more exalted (*Hebrew*) 'Sabbath' rest; literally, 'cessation': rest from *work when finished* (Heb. 4:4), as God rested (Rev. 16:17)".[64]

So this is for now *and* the future. Howley describes it this way: "God's rest is not wholly some future goal to be attained, but it is a present reality to be enjoyed."[65] When Hebrews states that God rested (Heb. 4:10), it was not a rest from doing good but "from what He had been doing (i.e., His creative activity). And when a man enters into God's sabbath-rest he, too, must desist from what he has been doing—in this case, attempting to work out his own salvation."[66]

This is an important aspect of the home of God, this saving place of light and protection, this covering, this "secret place" where one can settle down and stay. How we "labour" to enter in is through those three means

---

63   Strong, s.v. "sabbatismŏs," 64.
64   Jamieson, 449.
65   G.C.D. Howley, *A New Testament Commentary* (London: Pickering & Inglis Ltd, 1969), 546.
66   Ibid.

outlined above: prophecy, priest, and prayer. Prophecy calls us, as in Hebrews 4:12, where, after the verse on labouring to enter into rest, we read, "For the word of God is quick, and powerful, and sharper than any two-edged sword, piercing even to the dividing asunder of soul and spirit, and of the joints and marrow, and is a discerner of the thoughts and intents of the heart." Scripture explains our need for an intermediary "high priest". And throughout is the consistent exhortation to prayer, from Genesis through to the penultimate verse of the Bible—the prayer, "come, Lord Jesus" (Rev. 22:20).

To get into God's place, we first need to enter our own devotional place of prayer, communion with God, and quality time seeking His face. Then we can connect with Him and find the real "place of the Most High", which is under His "shadow".

This is where His presence enters our soul, giving peace. We must create our own secret space in order to enter His secret place. Being born from above, we have right of admission and a measure of God's confirming peace and presence. We are changed and made anew, and He begins working within us. A continuous sense of His presence, however, does not always come automatically and must be accessed daily, not from works but through faith, by which we find an enduring relationship with Him. In the final verses—in the words of God Himself—we will hear more of this; it will become clearer as we go through our study. To begin, though, we must make a choice every day to sit down in His presence and abide throughout the day under His shadow, under His "feathers" and "wings", like a little bird trying to nestle into the mother bird as she spreads her wings and actively takes it under her feathers. The baby bird *knows* where to go for shelter and feels the comfort of being next to the mother but is only completely secure once *under* the wing.

God is like this. While we sense His abiding presence beside us and His Spirit inside us, our ultimate security and peace remains under that wing. And the imagery is apt, for the experience is one of closeness. Some falter, though, keeping their problems because they have only gotten *beside* the source of solutions and not *under* it. God spreads His "wings" as His love compels Him, and our need constrains us to move towards Him while we sense His response and tenderness.

Psalm 63:1-2 captures this idea beautifully: "O God, thou art my God; early will I seek thee: my soul thirsteth for thee, my flesh longeth for thee in a dry and thirsty land, where no water is; To see thy power and thy glory, so as I have seen thee in the sanctuary".

CHAPTER 3

REFUGE AND FORTRESS

STROPHE TWO

"I will say of the LORD, He is my refuge and my fortress: my God;
in him will I trust." (v. 2)

THE PSALMIST NOW SPEAKS of himself. Both the beginning and
the ending of the verse have the key phrases, "I will say" and "will I trust".
The use of "I will" and "will I" occurs eight times in the psalm—here where
the believer is speaking, and in verses fourteen to sixteen where God is
speaking. The King James Version normally uses "shall" to indicate certainty
and "will" to indicate determination. Those who live in God's shelter, under
His shadow, will speak of Him and trust in Him. This idea connects with
Psalm 2's statement: "Blessed are all they that put their trust in him." And
what blessings they are, as we saw in our discussion of verse one.

The Hebrew word for "LORD" is Yahweh (YHWH or *Yehôvâh*[67]), the
covenantal and redemptive title God gave Himself in Exodus 3:14: "I AM THAT
I AM" (i.e., the Self-Existent or Eternal as revealed to Moses). And *Shadday*[68]
was the name, both covenantal and benedictive, when God appeared as "the
Almighty God" to Abraham in Genesis 17:1-8, "God Almighty" to Isaac in

---

67 Strong, s.v. "Yehôvâh," 47.
68 Strong, s.v. "Shadday," 113.

Genesis 28:3 and Jacob in Genesis 35:11,[69] and "the Almighty" throughout the book of Job. In the final book of the Bible, the book of Revelation, "Almighty" is found eight times, echoing the Hebrew.

"I will say that he is two things for me", says the writer: a refuge and a fortress. We could think of a fortress here also as a castle. Next in the text, the two (refuge and fortress) are summarised by the words "my God"[70]. "My God" is often used casually today by many as an exclamation, in breach of the third commandment; but the name was the first that God used in the Bible when in Genesis 1:1, God stated, "In the beginning God created the heaven and the earth". By using this name to speak of Himself as the mighty Creator of the universe, He showed the sum of Who He can be to us, completely trustworthy as our refuge and fortress. And it was used throughout Genesis 1 until chapter two, verse four, where, with the creation of man, He is called "LORD God".

In Psalm 91:2, we get both names also together in the same line: "I will say of the LORD . . . my God; in him will I trust". This is the possible origin of the phrase, "In God we trust" (see also Psalm 18:2). The word for trust speaks of taking refuge, being confident, secure, sure, hopeful, even careless in the positive sense of being free from worry[71]. The theme is all through the Psalms—for example, "in thee do I trust" (Psalm 143:8).

We do not know how YHWH was pronounced—perhaps "YéH-Whoa", or "YaHWeH". Literally, Jehoshuä, is Jesus' name, in which is reflected God's sacred name. In the sixteenth century, consonants were given for English pronunciation, and it became "YeHoVaH" and, eventually, the hybrid "Jehovah". It is mainly translated as "LORD", normally in capital letters in the Old Testament.

Titles of God, transliterated,[72] and beginning with this name include:

---

69   In the case of Abraham, Sarah, and Jacob also initiating name changes.
70   Strong, s.v. "ĕlôhîym," 12.
71   Strong, s.v. "bâṭach," 20.
72   "O.T. Names of God - Study Resources," Blue Letter Bible, Accessed 21 December, 2023, https://www.blueletterbible.org/study/misc/name_god.cfm.

1. YHWH Jireh   our Provider
2. Rapha   our Healer
3. Nissi   our Banner
4. Shalom   our Peace
5. Tsidkenu   our Righteousness
6. Shammah   our Presence
7. Adonai   our Sovereign / Master
8. Mekoddishkem   our Sanctifier
9. Sabaoth   the Lord of hosts
10. El Elyon   the Most High
11. Raah   our Shepherd
12. Elohim   our Creator

The metric rhythm of the first phrase of this verse—"I will say of the Lord"—is of two anapaestic beats (˘ ˘ /, ˘ ˘ /) (i.e., two unstressed syllables followed by one stressed syllable[73]), significant because it forms a perfect introduction, like a drum roll, to the main statement that makes up the rest of the verse. If read aloud, it should be according to the punctuation given, including with the appropriate pauses. To place it in its conversational setting, then, "I will say of the LORD, 'He is my refuge and my fortress: my God; in him will I trust'". This, along with the middle of verse nine—"who is my refuge"—is the only time the writer speaks of himself.

The robust and sweeping introductory statement of verse one, addressed to all who will hear and respond, is followed appropriately by this declaration of verse two. What he says he will say is a summary of the whole psalm and almost *all* he says of himself and all he *needs* to say, for it speaks of his whole reason for penning the psalm.

---

73   *Literary Devices*, s.v. "Anapest," Accessed 21 December, 2023, https://literarydevices.net/anapest.

CHAPTER 4

DELIVERED FROM SNARE AND PESTILENCE

STROPHE THREE (A)

"Surely he shall deliver thee from the snare of the fowler,
and from the noisome pestilence." (v. 3)

LEST WE DWELL TOO long on the first person, the narrative reverts back to the main focus of the psalm: "thee"—that is, you and me, the readers or hearers of the words of this revelation from God. Building on the last word ("trust") of the previous verse is the word "surely". The two words "surely" and "shall" both have the same initial consonant: /ʃ/—"sh" and this alliterative effect is enhanced by the /s/ of "snare".

A study of "surely" in the Psalms reveals that several Hebrew words are used. This one is also used in Psalm 112:6 in its description of the righteous: "Surely he shall not be moved forever". Psalm 23:6 uses a different term, as does Psalm 85:9: "Surely his salvation is nigh them that fear him". It does not matter which is used, though, because they are all alike. "Surely" means definitely and inevitably (e.g., Amos 3:7: "Surely the Lord GOD will do nothing, but he revealeth his secret unto his servants the prophets"). And we should take note of the fact that Jesus' final words in the penultimate verse of the Bible are "Surely I come quickly" (Rev. 22:20).

"Deliver" means to be snatched away from, plucked out of, preserved, rescued, or recovered from. I counted twenty-one Hebrew words for "deliver" in my concordance. This one has the sense of being whisked away immediately before falling into a trap and is used elsewhere in the Psalms, such as in Psalm 7:1 or Psalm 31:2, where the adverb "speedily" is added for further emphasis of the process of being snatched quickly out of trouble (see also Psalm 31:15). God is surely watching our steps, even when we are unaware of it.

The "fowler" is a metaphor for an enemy; and the world is full of them, including those who are perverse results of the Fall and, hence, enemies of humankind, plus dangerous doctrines and ideologies and leaders who have succumbed to the lust for power or have become opposed to any kind of belief in God. In whichever way it comes, the "fowler"—ensnarer or entangler—is an enemy to all. It refers, too, to the definitive foe, the fowler who traps with the aim of capturing first, then using, abusing, and killing.

While other words are used to translate "snare", this onomatopoeic noun[74] is used in the following verses to describe what the wicked do:

- "The wicked have laid a snare for me: yet I erred not from thy precepts" (Psalm 119:110)
- "The proud have hid a snare for me" (Psalm 140:5a)
- "Keep me from the snares which they have laid for me" (Psalm 141:9a)
- "In the way wherein I walked have they privily laid a snare for me" (Psalm 142:3b).

Another ensnarer is sin. Proverbs 7:23 compares a young man considering adultery to a bird rushing unknowingly into a trap. And the day of judgement, or any awful calamity, catches people at any time, like a snare: "For man also knoweth not his time; as the fishes that are taken in an evil net, and as the

---

74 Strong, s.v. "pach," 94.

birds that are caught in the snare; so are the sons of men snared in an evil time, when it falleth suddenly upon them" (Eccl. 9:12).

The concept is reiterated in the New Testament in Jesus' warnings in Luke 21:34-36:

> And take heed to yourselves, lest at any time your hearts be overcharged with surfeiting, and drunkenness, and cares of this life, and so that day come upon you unawares. For as a snare shall it come on all them that dwell on the face of the whole earth. Watch ye therefore, and pray always, that ye may be accounted worthy to escape all these things that shall come to pass, and to stand before the Son of man.

And in I Timothy 6:9, we read, "But they that will be rich fall into temptation and a snare". The word for "snare" meant a trap or a spring net; and its Greek equivalent in the Luke and I Timothy references indicated a trap using a noose, or a trick, stratagem, or snare[75]. We see it in Romans 11:9, quoting from David in Psalm 69:22: "Let their table become a snare before them: and that which should have been for their welfare, let it become a trap." That word "trap", from which is derived "the fowler" of Psalm 91:3, is also used in Proverbs 12:13: "The wicked is snared by the transgression of his lips". The words that people speak can become their own snares! "The fear of man bringeth a snare (Prov. 29:25), "but whoso putteth his trust in the LORD shall be safe" (Prov. 29:25). To be safe is described in Psalm 91:14, where God will set the godly "on high".

Of course, the ultimate "snarer" is Satan, whose snare is described in I Timothy 3:7: "Lest he [i.e., the novice: a new believer placed too soon in a position of authority] fall into reproach and the snare of the devil", and II Timothy 2:26a: "That they may recover themselves out of the snare of the devil"—the "they" describing "those who oppose themselves" by being overly disputatious (v. 25).

---

75   Strong, s.v. "pagis," 53.

In verse seven of Psalm 124, we come across it again: "Our soul is escaped as a bird out of the snare of the fowlers: the snare is broken, and we are escaped. Our help is in the name of the LORD, who made heaven and earth" (Psalm 124:7, 8).

Birds usually do not know what a trap is at first. But if they spy someone setting one and are wary of it from previous observation, others having gone that way and never having returned, then they might avoid it; for "in vain the net is spread in the sight of any bird" (Prov. 1:17). Also, if there is a visible threat such as a prowling cat, they will send out warning signals to other birds. If they are not familiar with the danger, however, then they go about their business without expecting any harm. But the snare is brutal, lethal, final, and most effective when unseen. It traps or kills in an instant and robs parents of offspring, offspring of parents, and companions of companions.

We are like the birds. Having a high IQ is no guarantee of avoiding all of life's snares; and being naturally discerning, cunning, or streetwise also affords no complete protection. Snares are hidden and operate with no warning. Thankfully, God is ahead of the play in everything. He can prevent us falling into a snare and can pull us out if we get trapped. He can deliver us. And if we find ourselves ensnared already, He can release us.

Perhaps, though, He warned us first, and then we disobeyed. If so, there may be little assurance that we will get out easily or even at all. Our only hope is that His grace is immeasurable. Psalm 124:7 above shows that the snare can be broken and escape is possible, for "our help is in the name of the Lord, who made heaven and earth" (v. 8). When we call on that name, deliverance out of the worst trouble and out of all unforeseen snares is possible.

The outdated English word "noisome"[76], used once in the New Testament and three times in the Old Testament, comes from "annoy" and is a shortened form of the old word "annoysome". Today, an annoyance is a bothering event or situation usually not particularly harmful, like a mosquito buzzing around our heads at night or someone drumming their fingers when we are trying

---

76   Translated from the original as "mischiefs" in Psalm 52:2.

to concentrate. But its older meaning was stronger, stemming from the Latin *in odiō*—"in hatred". And the Hebrew here implies something perversely rushing upon us.

"Noisome" is something noxious, harmful, putrid. So the strength of the phrase "noisome pestilence" is evident. A pestilence is physical but could also refer to moral poison, as when a society gives itself over to certain beliefs or acts (plagues upon the heart, as in Exod. 9:14). The first thought, however, is of a literal plague or disease moving through a population, or livestock, or farm crops.

Whether the term is used in its primary or in any other meaning, again God states that He will deliver us. While taking as many sensible precautions as we should—diet, hygiene, sanitation, etc., which are taken for granted— our first call is still for His protection, since a pestilence or plague can show little mercy even to the most fastidious. God delivers—both from the snares of the enemy and from the epidemic. Imagine a biologically destructive pestilence or plague rushing upon people but God's own being snatched away, preserved, and rescued. Psalm 91 is clearly about this happening. The believer in God need not fear pandemic, plague, or pestilence. One of the greatest Bible commentators, C.H. Spurgeon, wrote of this verse, "Faith by cheering the heart keeps it free from the fear which, in times of pestilence, kills more than the plague"[77]. We will see more about this in verses six and ten.

Psalm 91 does not use the most commonly used Old Testament word for "sickness" or "disease"[78]. Other words, used elsewhere, cover all kinds of sicknesses, both mild and serious, including some "exceeding great" and incurable (II Chron. 16:12; 21:18). There is a word for the diseases of Egypt, as in Deuteronomy 7:15 and 28:60—God's either taking them away or adding them to His people depending on their level of obedience to Him. And Psalm 103:3 states of God that He is the One "who healeth all thy diseases"[79].

---

77   Charles Spurgeon, "Psalm 91 by C. H. Spurgeon," Blue Letter Bible, Last Modified 5 Dec 2016, https://www.blueletterbible.org/Comm/spurgeon_charles/tod/ps091.cfm.

78   Strong, s.v. "chŏlîy," 39.

79   Strong, s.v. "tachâlû'," 123.

However, the two words used in Psalm 91 are translated only as "pestilence" and "plague", although both can also refer to other sicknesses and diseases. Protection is, indeed, promised, but the assurances would appear to be dependent on the *whole* of the psalm being operative in our lives.

In a dictionary, we sometimes find "plague" identified with "pestilence" and vice versa. So can Psalm 91 protect us from a cold or a flu epidemic? First, it will not protect you from wrong health decisions. However, it could apply for the immune-compromised, for whom even a cold or flu can potentially be as deadly as the plague; for God knows the predicament of those of weak constitutions for whom minor ailments can be serious. For the rest of the population, yearly influenzas normally help build natural herd immunity. But whether Divine protection will happen every time or all the time is another question. God *can* protect. Psalm 91 preaches protection from the serious diseases of plagues and pestilences—that is what it says.

The psalm itself, of course, does not protect, but its Divine Author can—and not only from disease. Stories have been told about army platoons claiming Psalm 91 for safety and then experiencing no casualties. Such stories need proof, but the idea is plausible; for where even a measure of faith has been exercised, nothing is impossible. God wrote the narrative, put it in poetic form as a *précis* of the message of salvation, and created it not as a magic wand but as an invitation to a relationship. Herein is the message of redemption from man's fall, from which disease and sickness came. It starts with "he" (put yourself there) and ends with salvation, with everything relevant to that in between.

Psalm 91 is like a breath of fresh, clean air after coming out of a suffocating environment. We see and hear a message from eternity that pestilences and plagues were never meant to exist and are abhorrent to the God Who created everything perfect. The protection He promises is what the psalm speaks of and offers no alternative to its validity. Either the Word is completely irrelevant—a useless piece of writing, despite all its wonderful literary devices—or it is true from beginning to end.

Second Timothy 3:16 asserts the truthfulness of the entire scope of the Scriptures: "All scripture is given by inspiration of God, and is profitable for doctrine, for reproof, for correction, for instruction in righteousness." We need only to read it correctly. And that is why getting some understanding of the original languages and then comparing Scripture with Scripture is so useful. The "snare of the fowler" and the "noisome pestilence" are equally threatening to every human and always will be while this world remains as it is. Restoration is what we long for and look for; and in the meantime, we trust the God Whose truth is our "shield and buckler" (coming in the next verse) and Who seeks to restore us to a relationship with Him.

To sum up the second main theme of the verse, "plague" and "pestilence" sometimes equate with "sickness" and "disease" in the Bible, although not always. Exodus 11:1 speaks of one more plague, the tenth, on the Egyptians (in other words all the other nine were also plagues, even though some were not physical sicknesses, such as the plague of flies). In I Kings 8:37, "pestilence" is joined with "mildew" and "locust", verse thirty-eight speaking of every man knowing "the plague of his own heart". And Zechariah 14:15 tells us about a plague afflicting animals. The New Testament gives even wider application of "plague", as in the book of Revelation. All this should be kept in mind so that the references to plague or pestilence in Psalm 91 do not get narrowed down to only one interpretation. They are interchangeable. But the fact that Psalm 91 uses terms three times to describe this reveals that *much* is covered by its promises.

Grammatically, verse three has one adverb ("surely"), one verb phrase ("shall deliver"), a preposition ("from" twice), two noun phrases ("the snare of the fowler" and "the noisome pestilence), and two personal pronouns ("he" and "thee"). And from here until verse fourteen, where God takes over the narrative, the psalmist addresses "you" (i.e., you the reader, the believer) broken only by that brief phrase in verse nine, reminding us of his personal declaration from verse two. Hence we have:

"He" (v. 1) → "I" (v. 2) → "you" (vv. 3-13) → "he" (vv.14-16).

COVERED AND EQUIPPED: TRUST AND TRUTH

STROPHE THREE (A) (CONT.)

"He shall cover thee with his feathers, and under his wings shalt thou trust:
his truth shall be thy shield and buckler." (v. 4)

THE VERSE EMPLOYS TWO metaphors. The first is of homeliness, security, and comfort, with rustic imagery of a bird actively protecting its young, its chicks keeping themselves under its wings. The second relates to safety in life's battles, with the imagery of God's truth being like protective armour. Both metaphors apply to those in covenant relationship with the Lord.

Under the feathers of the parent, the hatchling finds safety and warmth. Many birds do this—such as chickens, pigeons, and wood storks—which cover their young to protect them from the sun.[80] When the fledglings have grown, parent birds do not need to protect them in this way. Hence, the analogy can be taken only so far and would break down if we were to assume that one day, God might throw us out of the nest, which, of course, is not even suggested. Rather, under His wings we can trust Him forever and in our lifetime relax and rest secure and confident. Jesus said, "Except ye be

---

80   "Birds of the Bible—Trusting under the Wing," Lee's Birdwatching Adventures Plus Birdwatching from a Christian Perspective, 9 January 2013, https://leesbird. com/2013/01/09/birds-of-the-bible-trusting-under-the-wing.

converted, and become as little children, ye shall not enter into the kingdom of heaven" (Matt. 18:3), indicating how we are to trust that God will keep us safe under His feathers and His wings.

The wings speak also of healing. Jesus is the "Sun of righteousness", Who arises "with healing in his wings" (Mal. 4:2). Malachi was speaking of Jesus' first coming, for never before then had healing of the kind He performed taken place on such a scale either in ancient Israel or anywhere in the world. That healing and the forgiveness He acquired for us were foreseen by prophets who were looking even further ahead towards the third manifestation of the kingdom of God in the coming of the Messiah: "And the inhabitant shall not say, I am sick: the people that dwell therein shall be forgiven their iniquity" (Isa. 33:24), and "the eyes of the blind shall be opened, and the ears of the deaf shall be unstopped. Then shall the lame man leap as an hart, and the tongue of the dumb sing" (Isa. 35:5-7). All this happened during Jesus' ministry and in the time of the early church, evidence of and harbingers of the kingdom of God, as recorded in the book of Acts. Malachi 4:2 uses the identical word for wings as that used in Psalm 91, metaphorical also of the curative "wings" of Jesus.

Many verses illustrate this wonderful theme. Boaz spoke of Ruth, that she had come to trust under the wings of the LORD God of Israel (Ruth 2:12). David prayed that God would hide him under the shadow of His wings and spoke of his trust "in the shadow of thy wings" (Psalm 17:8; 57:1). Psalm 36:7, as we saw in relation to verse one, stated that due to the excellence of God's lovingkindness, "The children of men put their trust under the shadow of thy wings". Any believer, especially in times of calamity, can find spiritual security under God's "wings". In Psalm 61:4, the psalmist confessed that he would "trust in the covert of thy wings"; and in Psalm 63:7, he exclaimed that because God had been his help, he would rejoice "in the shadow of thy wings". Clearly, it is a place of comfort, safety, and rejoicing.

Jesus, in line with the heart of God for the people of Jerusalem, exclaimed, "O Jerusalem, Jerusalem, thou that killest the prophets, and stonest them which are sent unto thee, how often would I have gathered thy children together, even as a hen gathereth her chickens under her wings, and ye would not! Behold, your house is left unto you desolate" (Matt. 23:37, 38).

Here is the heart of the Father and of Christ and a glimpse of the cross. These were those Jesus was going to die for not much later—for the whole world, ultimately, but for these His people in the first instance. In that statement is an anticipation of the cross: "thou that killest the prophets . . . and ye would not!". They had a choice. Imagine a baby bird wanting to be independent and to get out from under the cover of its mother's wings, but here they had not even wanted to enter the place of shelter to start with. Jesus said, "How often would I have . . .", but the people, self-willed, "would not!". And because of that, their house was left "desolate". While literally fulfilled in AD 70, the verb "is" meant that they were *already* desolate spiritually. They had made the choice to reject the truth of the prophets and the One Who said that He was the Truth. So we can voluntarily place ourselves under His wings.

The Hebrew word for "cover", as in "cover thee with his feathers", is also used in Exodus 33:22, where God said that He would put Moses in the cleft of a rock and cover him with His hand as He passed by, and in Job 40:22, where God speaks of the trees covering the creature "behemoth" ("the shady trees cover him with their shadow"). It implies being fenced in or covered over, symbolic of protection.

Under these "feathers" and "wings", we trust. To trust is to confide in, have hope in, or take refuge in (see Psalm 61:4). The original word[81], used also in Psalm 2:12b, appears to have rather more of a sense of hurry than the "trust" of verse two, which meant quiet confidence and security, making the depiction of a chick scurrying to the protection of its parent's wings complete.

The feathers and the wings speak also of being at home under the safe Fatherhood of God, where one may always stay. While abiding there in spirit, however, we must still go out into the battle of daily life and into the spiritual

---

81   Strong, s.v. "châçâh," 41.

fight for our faith and for truth. Hence, the second half of this verse follows on from the first with a different metaphor suitable to the theme of our engagement with life in the world. His truth is our shield, a defensive device that, in a skirmish or war, protects us from our enemies' offensive weapons. Also, it is a shield from extreme elements as with a canopy protecting us from the hot sun, driving rain, hail, or snow. In the Old Testament, the word used most often for "truth" means stability, certainty, truth, and trustworthiness[82].

The translations of shield and buckler are sometimes interchangeable in meaning as several words can describe both. One use of "buckler" was in reference to a small, round defensive shield traditionally worn on the left arm to help in the thrust and parry of smaller fights, a suitable size for archers to have on hand, as used by the Benjamite archers in II Chronicles 14:8 (transl. "shields") and in II Chronicles 23:9, Psalm 18:30, and Proverbs 2:7 (transl. "buckler"). These small shields were useful for hand-to-hand fighting but not for larger battles. Other words for "buckler" have different meanings, such as a lance in I Chronicles 12:8, or a large shield, possibly hooked or spiked, as in Psalm 35:2 (translated "buckler" and "target" in II Chronicles 14:8).

The Psalm 91 word for "buckler", however, is not used elsewhere and refers to a surrounding means of protection, covering most or all of the body almost like chainmail. The preceding noun "shield" means a large shield. Although the distinction between the two Hebrew words may be a little difficult for us to fully grasp today, the repetition of the theme of defence—a typical biblical double—strengthens the theme that God's truth will protect from every attack those who trust in Him.

Again, for emphasis, God's truth has come to us in twos as it does in other places in Scripture (sometimes also in threes or more). Here, the verse gives us feathers and wings in the first part and shield and buckler in the second.

---

82   Strong, s.v. "'emeth," 14.

CHAPTER 6
FEARLESS

STROPHE THREE (B)

"Thou shalt not be afraid for the terror by night; nor for the arrow that flieth by day; Nor for the pestilence that walketh in darkness; nor for the destruction that wasteth at noonday. A thousand shall fall at thy side, and ten thousand at thy right hand; but it shall not come nigh thee." (vv. 5-7)

SPEAKING OF FOUR MATTERS *not* to fear; these two verses offer examples of situation and time—night and day, darkness and noonday, terror and arrow, pestilence and destruction (again in doubles)—both animate and inanimate threats.

The grammatical similarity (with double-syllables and the double consonant "rr" in the middle) of the nouns "terror" and "arrow" indicates the use of poetic devices in the translation. Both verses use contrast—"night" versus "day"; "darkness" versus "noonday"—each couplet starting with the theme of the invisible—"terror" / "pestilence"; "night" / "darkness"—and ending with the visible—"arrow" / "destruction"; "day" / "noonday".

The first context in which we are not to be afraid (i.e., not have fear) is the night. And this "terror", which we have considered previously, is from the verb for being startled as from a sudden alarm[83]—like a bird getting trapped in a snare. The sense, however, with its connotations of fear and terror, is

---

83 Strong, s.v. "pâchad," 94.

stronger than only being startled. Night is when people, particularly the weak and vulnerable, often feel apprehensive—perhaps fretting over threats made in the daytime—and it is when nightmares sometimes come. Yet "night" can also be symbolic of stress, uncertainty, darkness, loneliness, and worry (a form of fear), none of which need be dreaded by the secret-place dweller, who will be unafraid of nighttime threats, whether real or imagined, *or* of daytime troubles. As David said in Psalm 4:8, "I will both lay me down in peace, and sleep: for thou, LORD, only makest me dwell in safety" (see also Psalm 127:2).

The believer in the midst of these calamities is not in a place of contemplative retreat, but out there in the world—and yet not *of* it. The flying arrow is a normal feature of the day. It could be an unknown hazard, a potential threat, an unexpected encounter, a negative comment, someone with a grudge or a vendetta, or spiritual darts coming in various guises that Satan, his cohorts, and his demon hordes aim at the believer. But the followers of God are discerning, identifying them and dealing with them from God's resources, with their heart in the right place—free of unforgiving bitterness or resentment. While the reference was to real arrows—real weapons—the figurative aspect is seen in its use elsewhere, as in:

- "For lo, the wicked bend their bow, they make ready their arrow upon the string, that they may privily shoot at the upright in heart" (Psalm 11:2, "privily" means secretly, in darkness and obscurity)
- "My soul is among lions . . . even the sons of men, whose teeth are spears and arrows, and their tongue a sharp sword" (Psalm 57:4)
- "Hide me from the secret counsel of the wicked; from the insurrection of the workers of iniquity: Who whet their tongue like a sword, and bend their bows to shoot their arrows, even bitter[84] words: That they may shoot in secret at the perfect" (Psalm 64:2, 3, 4a).

---

84 "Bitter" is mârâh, the state of the waters of Marah in Exodus 15:23 and also how Naomi felt when she and Ruth came to Bethlehem—"call me not Naomi, call me Mara, for the LORD hath dealt bitterly with me" (Ruth 1:20). It is also the root of the name "Mary".

The enemy's arrows need not touch those who are protected from "the terror by night" and "the arrow that flieth by day". Although anxiety will occasionally occur (and with justification), God's grace can mitigate it. We all need prayer, encouragement, and support from others, along with Divine grace. In Psalm 6:6 (in contrast to Psalm 4:8), David stated, "I am weary with my groaning; all the night make I my bed to swim; I water my couch with my tears." His bed "swims" from his copious tears, and then he goes to his couch and "waters" that, too, stating that his "eye is consumed because of grief; it waxeth old because of all mine enemies" (v. 7). He did not give up faith, though, for "The LORD hath heard my supplication; the LORD will receive my prayer" (v. 9). In communing with the Lord, David found mercy (Psalm 4:4). Jesus said, "In the world ye shall have tribulation: but be of good cheer; I have overcome the world" (John 16:33b), and He sometimes spent all night in prayer in the Garden of Gethsemane, where He prayed intensely before His impending trial and crucifixion. Yet earlier in His ministry (Mark 4:35-41), He was sleeping soundly in the middle of a storm on the Sea of Galilee, a visible illustration of Psalm 4:8.

God "will ever be mindful of his covenant." He always sends redemption to His people (Psalm 111:5, 9). Hence, neither "terror" nor "arrow" need make us fearful.

The "pestilence" is not figurative but means a plague or any threatening virus, epidemic, or pandemic, as seen before in verse three. The theme is three times in this psalm. But "pestilence" can also apply to the spread of a plague through a farmer's crops, plodding steadily, stealthily, step by step, in "darkness". The "destruction", however, *is* visible, because midday makes everything noticeable. The sun is at its height, and nothing is easily hidden as in the night. Yet this destruction is unexpected, as with a natural catastrophe like an earthquake or a man-made upheaval like a regional conflict or an economic crash. This word is found only three times in the Old Testament: here in Psalm 91, in Isaiah 28:2 ("a destroying storm"), and in Deuteronomy 32:24 ("bitter destruction").

With these four examples from verses five and six—the nighttime terror, the daytime arrow, the hidden pestilence, the noonday destruction—though the overall context of the psalm is one of complete protection, the verse is not saying that "you will be fully protected from" but rather, "you shall not be afraid of". The primary promise is protection from fear itself. Though threats may come, fear is needless; and panic and alarm unnecessary. This does not contradict what is already stated here or in other parts of the psalm—namely, that we also have protection (see below in verse seven: "it shall not come nigh thee" and ten: "There shall no evil befall thee"). But God looks at our commitment. The three persecuted Hebrew boys, when threatened with the fiery furnace by King Nebuchadnezzar during the Babylonian captivity, answered, "If it be so, our God whom we serve is able to deliver us from the burning fiery furnace, and he will deliver us out of thine hand, O king. But if not, be it known unto thee, O king, that we will not serve thy gods, nor worship the golden image which thou hast set up" (Dan. 3:17-18).

The addition of the words "but if not" allowed for the possibility of their *not* being rescued by God, even though they had twice affirmed unshakeable faith in His ability to deliver. This portrayed the paradox of faith faced by believers throughout the ages and the kind of confidence reflected in Psalm 91:5 to "not be afraid". The individual who fully trusts God is one who will "not be afraid of evil tidings: his heart is fixed, trusting in the LORD. His heart is established, he shall not be afraid" (Psalm 112:7, 8a). Many Scriptures support the concept of God's people, in covenantal relationship with Him, coming under His protection. Consider the whole of the exodus of the Hebrews from Egypt and the ten plagues that affected the Egyptians but not God's people or the small number of Egyptians who took heed to the warnings (Exod. 9:20, 21). God oversaw His people's deliverance: "And the blood shall be to you for a token upon the houses where ye are: and when I see the blood, I will pass over you, and the plague shall not be upon you to destroy you, when I smite the land of Egypt" (Exod. 12:13).

But terror, arrows, pestilence, and destruction—all extremes—will not come near the believer; the psalm says as much in the next four verses. In the wilderness, Israel had no means of protection other than God—no rescue helicopters, hospitals, medical centres, Red Cross, Doctors Without Borders, medical staff, surgeons, or nurses. They had God's laws, though, including dietary and sanitary laws, which served them well when they were diligent to keep them. And God was still their Healer and Deliverer. They needed Him for what they had no control over, as do we today. And on that score, nothing differs. That is why—although with modern amenities and advanced medical procedures, drugs, sanitation, clean water, etc.—we still need Psalm 91. We still need God because not only is it not always possible to gain access to those facilities and amenities, but threats will always exist—new, unknown, undealt with yet by modern medicine. Epidemics, bio-weapons, or any other threats— all are covered in this psalm which remains relevant today. We need fear none of them.

The verses dealing with the matter of sickness and disease are three, six, and ten; and the words again are, respectively, pestilence, pestilence again, and plague. Divine healing or "divine health" has been controversial over the years, but some aspects remain incontrovertible. Being fallen creatures, we naturally, over time, become subject to aches and pains; but God has shown time and again that health is often conditional upon obedience. The first fourteen verses of Deuteronomy 28, with its beatitudes, include clear statements describing how much is contingent upon obedience to God. There it is primarily referring to the health of a nation. But nations are made up of individuals. David, speaking of the One Who considers the poor, gives assurance of deliverance in times of trouble, preservation of life, blessing now, and safety from enemies: "The LORD will deliver him in time of trouble. The LORD will preserve him, and keep him alive; and he shall be blessed upon the earth; and thou wilt not deliver him unto the will of his enemies. The LORD will strengthen him upon the bed of languishing; thou wilt make all his bed in his sickness" (Psalm 41:1-3).

Verse three states that "in his sickness" (as happens occasionally), God will strengthen him, providing both relief and remedies, and thus "make all his bed". But we are also assured that the name of Jesus is above every power on earth, including sickness, and that God's resurrection power is within those who trust Him. Romans 8:11 offers some insight into interpreting these ideas and helps us gain a balanced perspective from Scripture: "But if the Spirit of him that raised up Jesus from the dead dwell in you, he that raised up Christ from the dead shall also quicken your mortal bodies by his Spirit that dwelleth in you."

So what about those with chronic illness, who have debilitating conditions, or who had a terrible accident prior to coming to faith and must live the rest of their lives with the result, or who are bed-bound or stricken by physical pain—perhaps even *after* becoming believers—or the severely or mildly disabled? Could this psalm, or the psalter itself, be relevant to them? Is God speaking to them as to others? I believe He is.

For everyone—in varying degrees—suffers from the consequences of the Fall. Whether or not we had a say in what has happened or are rueing past decisions which brought trouble, Psalm 91 stands not only for the whole but for all the broken, sick, damaged, and hurting, and for anyone who chooses to believe God still cares, whatever may have befallen them. All of us are special. And there is the secret place, the place of hope where evil cannot crush, the pledge that pestilence and plague will be stayed in their tracks and never come near; the assurance that God can be called upon, hears, and answers; the surety that angels will keep us "in all our ways", that it is not over, not hopeless. God is a Refuge and Fortress; His truth is our shield, and in Him we trust. The lion, adder, and dragon *can* be crushed and the believer set "on high" by knowing God's name. And he or she will surely see God's salvation.

Tragically, some psalms, such as Psalm 23, are often used as a tack-on after life is done, written on the back of a funeral service sheet. However, they were not originally written solely for mourners or for the dead but for the living, as was Psalm 91. Keeping Scripture only for funerals feeds people's distrust about why it exists at all. It is like saying, "Write that verse on the back of my funeral service sheet or sing it as a hymn, but while I am alive I will regard it all as totally irrelevant". No Christian, regardless how battered and bruised, thinks this way. The Word is for now. So, too, is the "balm of Gilead" (Jer. 8:22).

Sometimes, the God Who miraculously heals also—or instead—provides us with "means" which vary according to need. From a co-worker's recommendation, for many years I have been able to use an effective plant remedy for a minor ailment. "It was when people were suffering from the result of poisoned water in a well; and Jehovah revealed to Moses the healing branch to be put into the well. He used means."[85] Whether a miraculous event or an equally miraculous revelation to Moses that this particular "branch" or tree had natural cleansing and sanitising qualities, we do not know, though in one sense it does not matter, as either way here was a gift from God for the healing of His people. The bottom line is "The LORD shewed him a tree" (Exod. 15:25). Nowadays, many diseases can be avoided by treating water with chemicals and filtration; at that time, however, they had no such knowledge or means. But they had God.

The mention of the tree is significant because the Bible narrative begins with trees—the tree of the knowledge of good and evil and the tree of life—and it ends with a tree whose leaves are for the healing of nations (Rev. 22:2). In between is the "tree" of Calvary— "Cursed is everyone that hangeth on a tree" (Gal. 3:13)—by which we are redeemed and made recipients of "the blessing of Abraham . . . that we might receive the promise of the Spirit through faith" (Gal. 3:14). As the tree cast by Moses into the waters at Marah made the waters sweet, so are we saved by Calvary's tree, our hearts also being "made sweet".

Deuteronomy 20:19 states, "The tree of the field is man's life". The revelation of the tree at Marah was followed by a promise: "If thou wilt diligently hearken to the voice of the LORD thy God, and wilt do that which is right in his sight, and wilt give ear to his commandments, and keep all his

---

85   G. Campbell Morgan. *Great Chapters of the Bible* (Old Tappan: Fleming H Revell Co., 1935), 79.

statutes, I will put none of these diseases upon thee, which I have brought upon the Egyptians: for I am the LORD that healeth thee" (Exod. 15:26).

The Saviour, through His sufferings, with the crown of thorns being placed on His head and being whipped and dying on the cross, also brought us a covenant, some of which sounds comparable to that Marah covenant. For "by whose stripes ye were healed" (I Peter 2:24, taken from Isa. 53:5-6) speaks of healing. This covenant of spiritual redemption primarily refers to our relationship with God being healed, its main context being that we are returned to God as sheep to the Shepherd (v. 25). As a result of His wounding, bruising, chastisement, and stripes (Isa. 53:5), "we are healed", our being dead to sin and able to live righteously by Jesus' bearing our sins "in his own body on the tree" (I Peter 2:24). The healing is the "sweetness" whereby our "Marah"—our bitterness through sin and death—is made sweet by the life of Christ imparted to us by the Holy Spirit. Part of this whole context is also the fact that Isaiah describes *real* physical wounds, bruises, chastisements, and stripes—hence, the suggestion of physical healing too for believers. This is confirmed in Matthew 8:17. And in Isaiah 53:4, "griefs" is the word for sicknesses or anxieties.[86] Psalm 103:3 stated of God that He "healeth all thy diseases".

Concluding that this was all only for the Old Testament is a mistake. Also incorrect is to state that all miracles ceased with the death of the last apostle. First, miracles were not confined to apostles, even during the life of Jesus (see Mark 9:38-39). Second, on the nature of apostles,[87] the main use of the term (i.e., the Twelve plus Paul) relates to the three qualifications of those forming the foundation of the Church (Eph. 2:20): first a witness of the resurrected Lord (I Cor. 15:7-9); second, a ministry characterised by "signs, and wonders, and mighty deeds" (II Cor. 12:12); and third, acquaintance with the whole life and work of Jesus through association (i.e., a disciple, see Acts 1:21-22). Wider use of the word, translated several times as "messengers", included Barnabas,

---

86   Strong, s.v. "chŏlîy," 39.
87   Strong, s.v. "apŏstŏlŏs," 15.

Silvanus, some unnamed others, and Epaphroditus, Andronicus, Junia, and Timothy, several of whom, as far as we know, did not fulfil all the three qualifications for an apostle, yet were still named as such.

The list of the eight gifts in I Corinthians 12:28-31, which begins with apostles, was not of chronology but of priority (i.e., we still have teachers in the church, "governments" or directorships, and evangelists and pastors as in Ephesians 4:11), which opens the way for further application of the word in distinction from the original disciples alone; so, for example, consigning it to the Corinthian church only and then in turn trying to apply I Corinthians 13 (the "love chapter") to today would be inconsistent.

The book of James encourages the sick to call the elders of the church for prayer. Healing—or, at least, some sort of relief—is the clear expectation following any confession of sin. If it was only for that era, then the rest of James' teaching would also come under question.

Yet our health is naturally dependent on individual strengths and weaknesses, experiences, genetic backgrounds, domestic and social environments, knowledge, and choices. Paul—who himself had witnessed and taken part in "special miracles", including powerful healings of the sick (Acts 19:11-12)—would likely have shared John's greeting wish for Gaius: "I wish above all things that thou mayest prosper and be in health" (III John 2). Yet Paul reminded us of some undeniable facts that "we have this treasure in earthen vessels, that the excellency of the power may be of God, and not of us", referring to the resurrecting power of God, and that "though our outward man perish, yet the inward man is renewed day by day . . . the things which are seen are temporal; but the things which are not seen are eternal" (II Cor. 4:7, 16, 18).

So while the final verse of Psalm 91 seems to suggest that unbroken—or, at least, overall general health—till the day we die *may* be possible, as we will learn later, these verses five through seven are in the meantime affirming protection from pestilence and plague throughout our lives, within the context of relationship and obedience (Deut. 28:1-14).

How Christians in the Middle Ages and later dealt with the plague is another study. For every story, someone will bring a counter-story, for every testimony a counter-testimony; and there lies the challenge. Millions died, yet some recovered (explained by some researchers as being due, apparently, and, at least in some cases, to a human genetic variant named Delta 32). The reformer Ulrich Zwingli, in ministering to plague victims, fell ill but then recovered, and this appeared to deepen his faith, as he wrote "Lo, Satan strains to snatch his prey; I feel his grasp; must I give way? He harms me not, I feel no loss, For here I lie beneath Thy cross."[88]

Nicholson (2003)[89] also makes mention of Thomas Morton, a Church of England vicar who ministered to plague victims in York, England, in 1602. While other clergy escaped to their country mansions, Morton lived amongst the sick and dying, sometimes even sleeping in the same room. But he lived to ninety-five! We may speculate: Was it his genetics? Did he daily hold to Psalm 91? He would surely have claimed Jesus as his Saviour and Lord; and one would think that at some time in his life, he would have found his security in "the secret place of the Most High". Perhaps, too, though, relationship and obedience—again, strong features of the Gospel message, not to mention faith—could have been part of the equation. Others though might have considered him to have been simply reckless but lucky.

The angels sent "to keep thee in all thy ways" (v. 11) can heal, too, as angels can do if we consider the story of the pool of Bethesda in the New Testament (John 5:1-4). Or they might guide us to the best surgeon, medication, hospital, or place of care. They could also guide a God-honouring nation towards better ways of preserving and improving people's health. Our physical life is limited and our health by no means always perfect. From birth, our bodies are constantly subjected to challenges and assaults; and we

---

88   Peter Hammond, *The Greatest Century of Reformation* (Cape Town: Christian Liberty Books, 2006), 61.
89   Adam Nicholson, *Power and Glory: Jacobean England and the Making of the King James Bible* (London: Harper Collins Publishers, 2003).

start aging from quite early. We all carry microbes and pathogens (viruses, bacteria, fungi, and parasites) which also surround us, a potential exception being a pristinely clean hospital environment with expensive equipment to maintain it—but that, too, is temporary. A single drop of sea water carries millions of viruses. And while our own bacterial bugs help build our resistance, infectious and opportunist viruses try to take advantage of those with weak immune systems—which for all of us tend to deteriorate near the end of our lifespans.

We cannot help but age, the whole fallen world being subject to the second law of thermodynamics and the law of entropy, by which all matter eventually winds down. Therefore, while some ailments can be resisted through exercise, supplements, or medicine, much is still beyond our control.

That, however, is why we have this psalm; because according to it and many other Scriptures, God is aware of and concerned about matters over which we have little or no control. Many of them need not harm us, provided we are in the place of open relationship with Him, with our spiritual "accounts" clear, our hearts pure, and our souls and minds unsullied by "the world, the flesh, and the devil". While being imperfect, we do whatever is possible to stay in that right association with Him and with others and to keep ourselves in as good a state of health as possible, physically, mentally, and—via the secret place—spiritually. Whatever assails us that God knows is beyond our ability to control or outside of our awareness is the focus of this psalm. Psalm 91 is from the spiritual—the "supernatural"—realm. What it speaks of is the possibility of God's shelter from the worst of the fallen world's challenges, even into our old age.

"Plague" and "pestilence" are mentioned thrice. And as we saw earlier, the main word for "sickness" in the Old Testament is not used in Psalm 91. That does not mean that the protection of God does not apply to other sicknesses, though, for God spoke to Israel that He would "take sickness away from the midst of thee" (Exod. 23:25). Many uses of the word are connected to the covenantal issue of whether people have obeyed God. Sleep and the Sabbath are God's provision to renew us, although we sometimes need extra rest. Our health can also depend on how we look after ourselves. For example, expecting God to protect us if we are careless with food preparation or general hygiene and sanitation is unreasonable and impractical. God's protection *may* cover situations in which we have unknowingly partaken of something unhealthy or where hazards exist of which we are unaware. And we sometimes misjudge our strength or overwork; the young do not always look after themselves as they should; the old, usually frailer, neglect themselves and need help; and middle-agers occasionally burn themselves out in the fast lane. Others live in squalid poverty, surrounded by disease and death.

But even in a "perfect" environment, people do not necessarily take care of their health. Simple risks exist constantly, both mild and serious. We may forget a jacket in wet weather and get caught in the rain, for example. When life gets out of balance, we get messages to change our lifestyle or diet or seek for extra rest and mental refreshment. Our "outward man" will still ultimately perish, but what is promised in Scripture is the extra factor of God's power with us. His defence and healing remain as real and relevant as they did three thousand years ago. So with wisdom from above, we can manage ourselves more effectively and more pleasingly to God.

Considered from a non-religious viewpoint, the promises of Psalm 91 might be seen as unrealistic. But though clearly beyond the natural, these remarkable verses cannot be expunged from Scripture or ignored. Even for those who argue for its being all for an earlier era, inevitably, understandably, *someone* is going to pick out some of these verses and try to apply them. Indeed, all Christians would argue that God is their Refuge and their Trust. It was not written for a perfect world but an imperfect one in which an omnipotent, omniscient Being loves us and draws us to Himself. It is not simply a piece of prose to be dismissed or disparaged. So if we accept it as wonderful literature, why not also uphold it as God's Word? In summary, then, according to this psalm, plague and pestilence need not come near the believer's dwelling.

Finally, regarding the other half of verse six, the "destruction that wasteth at noonday", literally that swells up or devastates during the daytime, again there is no need for fear. It could come from any direction, but the child of God who is specifically sheltering in the secret place is safe.

Verses five and six form one complete sentence and are noteworthy in relation to the psalm's literary style. I will digress briefly here, using a few technical terms, into some poetic features of this sentence, touching on rhythm, metre, and the word flow, with consideration of how the translators may have thought as they rendered this beautiful psalm into English.

Language—poetic language in particular—like music, has rhythm, including beats and metre. So verse five has two lines, the first an anapaestic tetrameter (four anapaestic feet[90]), and the second a dactylic trimeter (three dactylic feet) ending with a single stressed syllable. Both lines have four stressed syllables, and the second line is a rhythmic reversal of the first.

Thou shalt **not/** be a**fraid/** for the **terr/**or by **night**;

nor for the/ **a**rrow that/ **fli**eth by **/day**;

The next clause (v. 6) of the sentence has a dactylic feel in both lines (parallel to the second line of verse five). Each line of verse six finishes with a trochee. Both lines, as in verse five, have four stressed syllables, and both have defining relative clauses beginning with "that". The subject nouns

---

90   A "foot" in poetry is a single unit of metre or rhythm. Each line of poetry has a certain number of feet.

"pestilence" and "destruction", being trisyllabic, both form rhythmic triplets. And each line has a disyllabic verb starting with "w".

Nor for the/ **pest**ilence that/ **walk**eth in/ **dark**ness;

nor for the/ de**struc**tion that/ **was**teth at/ **noon**day.

Further, each syllable of the nouns "**d**ark-**n**ess" and "**n**oon-**d**ay" in the adverbial phrases have primary consonants that together form a palindrome, i.e., **d—n**: **n—d**.

The next verse (seven) has a first clause beginning with a dactylic dimeter (two feet) and ending on a stressed syllable, "A/ **thou**sand shall/ **fall** at thy/ **side**". And the poetry appears to cease from there on.

This mixing of poetry and prose in the King James Version provides for variety, helping the psalm move forward as an integral whole. Of course, if *all* the Bible were in strict or even loose poetic form, its impact would likely be lost. But it may still be versified in hymns or recitations (e.g., the Scottish psalter), as hymn writers have done for centuries.

While the biblical Hebrew also shows evidence of poetic devices, here we are focusing on the English. More could be said about prosody—how it can be read aloud with correctly-stressed syllables, intonation, and pauses, as it deserves to be if read publicly. We could narrate the sentence of verses five and six, for example, with natural spoken rhythms while also tapping out its sixteen beats. A simple rhythmic pulse of one beat per second (e.g., crotchet equals sixty) would allow this and many other passages to be read as "poetic prose" (prose with poetic features). Every reading will be different, rendering any single transcription redundant; but by tapping the rhythm and reading audibly at pace, we can get the idea. Generally, that pace should be even, with a beat or two inserted between verses as suits.

The real question is not as much about the distinction between poetry and prose as about why it reads the way it does in contrast to, for example, a novel or a newspaper article. I have highlighted verses five and six of Psalm 91 for their obvious poetic value because the psalm is a song and a Divine poem; and we are free to explore its beauty and arrange it as we wish in our own language as the translators have done, providing it does not deviate from the original meaning.

Whether what we have here is the brilliance of the translators, the inspiration of the Spirit, or both, remains another question. Either way, of these we may be sure, the arrow *will* fly by day, the pestilence *will* walk in darkness, and the destruction *will* waste at noonday—but we need not fear, for it will not come near, as we are reminded of in the next verse: "A thousand shall fall at thy side, and ten thousand at thy right hand; but it shall not come nigh thee" (vs. 7).

Continuing the illustration of what *not* to fear, here the wicked fall on both sides, but the cause of their fall does not come near the believer. The contrastive "but" is like the sun coming out of the clouds. "It shall not come nigh thee."

While uncertain which of the previous four scenarios applies—the night time "terror", the daytime "arrow", the "pestilence", or the "destruction"—or all of them, either way the believer is in between, in the thick of it, yet untouched.

Occasionally, biblical figures of speech are constructed from "thousand" and "ten thousand" as we see in the following examples:

- "Cattle on a thousand hills" (Psalm 50:10)
- "A day in thy courts is better than a thousand" (Psalm 84:10)
- "For a thousand years in thy sight are but as yesterday when it is past" (Psalm 90:4a)
- "The word which he commanded to a thousand generations" (Psalm 105:8b)
- "The law of thy mouth is better unto me than thousands of gold and silver" (Psalm 119:72).

The "ten thousand" is added for extra strength: "How should one chase a thousand, and two put ten thousand to flight" (Deut. 32:30), "that our sheep may bring forth thousands and ten thousands in our streets" (Psalm 144:13); and after David fought with Goliath, the women of Israel danced, taunting Saul in their song by insinuating that his military prowess was inferior to David's. "Saul hath slain his thousands, and David his ten thousands" (I Sam. 18:6, 7; 21:11).

"Thousand" and "ten thousand" are symbolic of sizeable figures. Joshua, Caleb, and Moses would have seen such numbers in the demise of the Egyptians in the fifth and sixth judgements and the deaths by plague of the rebellious Israelites (14,700 of them) in Numbers 16:49.

So the use of "thousands" and "ten thousands" in Psalm 91 is for emphasis. The psalmist has, on either side of him, large numbers of nonbelievers, all unprotected from the terror, arrows, pestilence, and destruction.

CHAPTER 7

THE REWARD OF THE WICKED

STROPHE THREE (C)

"Only with thine eyes shalt thou behold and see the reward of the wicked." (v. 8)

THE SIMPLE MESSAGE HERE is that you will be able to see what happens to evil people. The King James Version puts it simply—"only with thine eyes"—and of course, we may say, how else might we behold but with our eyes? The emphasis is on the fact that none of the four threats described in the previous verse will come near the believer; but he will be able to perceive what happens to those who, due to their wickedness, are outside God's protection.

What then will he see? With "behold" and "see" translated separately in the Hebrew, we have three references in one verse to the process of seeing: "eyes", "behold", and "see". "Eyes" means eyes. "Behold" is also sometimes translated "see", as in Psalm 92:11 and 94:9—that is to scan with the sense of looking intently at or deeply considering or to regard with pleasure, favour, or care.[91] Here it could mean behold in the sense of seeing or considering, so not necessarily with the eyes. In other words, it could also be a process of deep thought requiring reflection and careful consideration beyond simply the physical act of seeing.

---

91   Strong, s.v. "nâbaṭ," 75.

"See" is the most frequently used word to describe seeing[92], but also with a range of associated meanings including to have experience of or to perceive or *cause* to see (as with "shew" in the final verse). Some examples include:

- Where God brought the animals to Adam "to see what he would call them" (Gen. 2:19)
- "Ye see the distress that we are in" (Neh. 2:17)
- "And see if there be any wicked way in me" (Psalm 139:24).

This verse calls for in-depth exegesis. What exactly would we expect to behold, see, observe, or have cause to reflect on here? A reward is normally what we get from a positive action, but also, negatively, a "reward" can be the consequence of a misdeed. And here, "reward" is clearly a metaphor of judgement, signifying retribution, punishment for evil, or evil befalling a wrongdoer ("the wicked"), consequent to their actions and choices.

Let us start our study of this verse with an interesting observation on God's character. In the book of Jeremiah, judgements are pronounced by God through the prophet over a number of areas and peoples, especially Judah, Egypt, the Philistines, the Moabites, the Ammonites, the Edomites, the Elamites, and Babylon; but God also expresses His Divine sorrow over the fact that judgement must take place (see Jeremiah 48:31-32). And neither are His people bidden to gloat over the demise of the ungodly but simply to "behold and see" (i.e., consider) because the Scripture also speaks of us requesting God to intervene on their behalf. From a New Testament perspective, too, believers are not generally called to rejoice over the fall of the wicked.

Some sections of the Bible, however, do seem to encourage it. The fifth and sixth judgements on Egypt were first the judgement of the "murrain" on their cattle, horses, camels, oxen, and sheep and second the judgement of boils or inflammations. After this, God said that He would send His "plagues

---

upon thine heart" (Exod. 9:14) and that He would "smite thee and thy people with pestilence; and thou shalt be cut off from the earth" (v. 15). All this because of Pharaoh's unrepentant heart. Moses and Israel beheld all this and later left Egypt and crossed the Red Sea. Then they rejoiced over their enemies' downfall. An old song based on it goes, "I will sing unto the Lord for He has triumphed gloriously, the horse and rider fell into the sea" (see Exod. 15:1, 21). So should we truly rejoice over the horse and rider getting thrown into the sea? Israel did. Moses sang, and his song inspired the women of Israel, under the leadership of the prophetess (and Aaron and Moses' sister), Miriam, to take up timbrels and to sing and dance, too.

The first part of Exodus might cause us to be careful about judging them. They had been enslaved by the Egyptians for hundreds of years, put to hard labour, oppressed, and finally chased to the Red Sea to what many thought would be certain slaughter. Moses' song looked ahead, too: "sorrow shall take hold on the inhabitants of Palestina" and, regarding the Edomites, Moabites, and Canaanites, "fear and dread shall fall upon them" (Exod. 15:14-17). In the flush of victory—God's victory—Moses predicted that those whose land they would enter forty years later would be trembling in their boots at the news. Was he getting carried away, or was it true that the news of God's favour to Israel was about to spread?

As we have seen, women sang of David's and Saul's victories over their enemies, reminding us of other passages such as when David rejoiced in II Samuel 22 over his enemies' demise. We should read the story in context. The II Samuel passage was a psalm which starts in many ways analogous to Psalm 91 and must be read in the framework of David's rise and constant conflict with those who opposed his kingship and any kind of God-honouring leadership. David was a warrior by nature but also had a deep and loving relationship with his Creator; and he had to live with the tension this created, as he could not be one without the other. Also, as in Moses' day and the days of Lot in Sodom, violent and immoral cultures of the area refused to countenance any

God-fearing culture such as Israel's was called by God to be. His instructions to His people should be seen in this light.

In contrast, in Matthew 5:12, the command of Jesus was for those being persecuted to rejoice, not over the downfall of their persecutors—for later in His discourse came the injunction to love one's enemies—but over the fact that their persecution was for the right cause. The kingdom of Heaven was theirs; a reward was waiting; and they were in the company of previously persecuted prophets. This was clearly persecution for their faith.

David, despite his background as the sling-wielding fighter for God, also prayed and fasted for some of his enemies when *they* were sick (Psalm 35:13, 14) as if they were a friend or a brother. But at the same time, he recognised that "the LORD preserveth the faithful, and plentifully rewardeth the proud doer" (Psalm 31:23). And although the word here for "rewardeth" is a different word than in Psalm 91, the sentiment is the same: God's "rewards" are according to whom He is dealing with. The God-fearer then may *observe* the retribution that God brings on the wicked as a warning to others.

It seems to go further than that, though. Referring to the godly man or woman in Psalm 112:8, David wrote that the godly "shall not be afraid, until he see his desire upon his enemies". Psalm 91 can help us to understand Psalm 112. After Psalm 91 is Psalm 92; and in verse eleven, not only the eyes but also the ears learn of God's judgement: "Mine eye also shall see my desire on my enemies, and mine ears shall hear my desire of the wicked that rise up against me." Since David also prayed and fasted for at least some of his enemies, what was this "desire"?

Vengeance is mentioned about thirty-eight times in the Old Testament and seven in the New. Psalm 35:1 begins, "Plead my cause, O LORD, with them that strive with me: fight against them that fight against me." While specific verses give us the substance, the whole psalm reveals the full meaning. David would have known the Exodus injunction to consider the welfare of one's enemies' animals ("thine enemy's ox", "the ass of him that hateth thee", Exod. 23:4-5), and clearly, by implication, to look out for the wellbeing of one's opponents, including respecting their legitimate human needs and the sanctity of their property. And though the "enemy" in Exodus 23 would more likely have been a fellow-countryman than a Philistine or a Canaanite, hypothetically, even the Philistine and Canaanite would not have been exempt from the right to respect, were they living next door. Here is the equivalent of Jesus' words to love your enemies. Leviticus 19:34 states, "The stranger that dwelleth with you shall be unto you as one born among you, and thou shalt love him as thyself; for ye were strangers in the land of Egypt".

An example of the fulfilment of Jesus' call to love one's enemy is when Martin Luther—who had referred to his staunch opponent the indulgence-selling Dominican friar Johann Tetzel as "a great ranter" and after hearing news that Tetsel was in his last days and ill—said, "When I found this out before his death, I comforted him with a letter, written benignly, asking him to be of good cheer and not to fear my memory".[93]

What, then, was the type of people David constantly had to deal with? These were surely not mildly unfriendly neighbours but implacable enemies and opponents of God, contrary to God's rule as with those in Psalm 2 who plotted against Him. David had to deal with people such as those mentioned in Psalm 35: "For without cause have they hid for me their net in a pit, which without cause they have digged for my soul" (35:7). Not only were they after him, but others, too. "They devise deceitful matters against them that are quiet in the land . . . This thou hast seen, O LORD" (vv. 20, 22). Those who are "quiet in the land" are those not causing anyone any trouble. But they, too, can be targets of the wicked. So there was legitimate cause for David's complaint which he lays out plainly before God, "Judge me, O LORD my God, according to thy righteousness . . . Let them be ashamed and brought to confusion together that rejoice at mine hurt" (vv. 24, 26).

---

93   Kurt Aland, *Martin Luther's 95 Theses* (Saint Louis: Concordia Publishing House, 1967), 30, 33.

These were cries for justice. God's response came in two succeeding psalms (37 and 38), where David preaches and teaches, God's voice being heard over his:

> Fret not thyself because of evildoers . . . Trust in the LORD and do good . . . Delight thyself also in the LORD . . . Commit thy way unto the LORD . . . Rest in the LORD . . . fret not thyself because of him who prospereth in his way, because of the man who bringeth wicked devices to pass. Cease from anger, and forsake wrath: fret not thyself in any wise to do evil. For evildoers shall be cut off: but those that wait upon the LORD, they shall inherit the earth. (Psalm 37:1, 3-5, 7-9)

Three times, "fret not" occurs. The final words quoted above ("they shall inherit the earth") form one of seven such promises, starting from verse three, regarding the matter of the "inheritance" of the earth as reiterated by Jesus in the third beatitude in Matthew 5:5. Hence, God's reply regarding the complaints of one of His faithful servants—"do not fret"; "trust in the Lord"; "commit your way to Him"; "rest in Him"; "do not be angry"; and "do not do evil".

Regarding vengeance, then—however one may consider the term—the Bible renders it as primarily God's prerogative. And most importantly, the call for retribution from the lips of godly prophets, priests, or kings is on behalf of the need for justice.

Some might see here attempts to fit human terms onto an eternal deity. However, human language is all we have, and a few words and phrases in our language do tackle such ideas. Take the word "holy", which could be applied to humans to a degree in reference to someone set apart for religious purposes; but ultimately, in its scriptural use for God, it refers to a concept *transcending* human experience or understanding. The same is true with vengeance, which for us may imply out-of-control rage and cruelty; but in denoting God, Who plainly stated, "Vengeance is mine", the same criteria cannot possibly be applied.

So we start to comprehend—though we may never do so fully—the concept of Divine "vengeance" by looking at God's dealings with people and nations over the span of history and by considering His words in passages such as these psalms or the writings of Moses, the prophets, or specific New Testament passages. He cannot be downsized to a soft, warm, and friendly Deity Who is perpetually sad that His creatures cannot sort themselves out and do what is right. Instead, God is offended (again, a human term) and grieved (another) by the violence and bloodshed He sees on earth. Writers like John in the book of Revelation can be sympathised with as they struggled to communicate in language, and did so well, what they saw in a world invisible to us here on earth.

So we have seen that while David prayed for his enemies, he also prayed "fight against them that fight against me" (Psalm 35:1); and "Let them be ashamed and confounded that seek after my soul: let them be turned backward and put to confusion, that desire my hurt" (Psalm 70:2). His sentiments can be understood, as in Psalm 139, where he says that he hated "with perfect hatred" those who spoke against God, hated God, rose up against Him, and took His name in vain (see verses 19-22). In times of intensity, he burst out, rightly or wrongly, with such requests to God. God had the final say, though, regarding how, when, or even if He would respond. Psalm 23 has the famous passage, "Thou preparest a table before me in the presence of mine enemies" (v. 5). Here, the tables are turned, and the psalmist's enemies seem to have the unpleasant experience of being forced to observe God's faithful follower being given a Divinely prepared meal!

Troubled as David was by evildoers, being a man of God, he had to learn not to take vengeance on his enemies when he had occasion and means to do so. A fascinating illustration of this learning process is in I Samuel 25, where we read of a man whose character matched his name—Nabal ("fool"—maybe a nickname but the only name given us of him), who was "churlish and evil in his doings".

Nabal was living in a thriving area named Carmel (not Mount Carmel but a place and town in Judea, south of Bethlehem the home of David) and he was himself prosperous. He had a wife named Abigail (meaning "source of joy"). David and his men were in the area and needing supplies, so David sent ten men out to greet Nabal and ask for his help. David's request was rudely declined, revealing Nabal's selfishness, stinginess, arrogance, and judgementalism. In colourful language, David vowed, rashly, to kill Nabal and all his men. This would, of course, have caused him future years of regret and more blood on his hands.

Nabal's wife, having gotten wind of what was happening, went out to greet David with supplies of bread, wine, dressed sheep, raisins, and figs. She was a negotiator *par excellence* and knew how men think. Her words to David in I Samuel 25:24-31 exemplify how to keep peace and negotiate. She began by advising David not to waste his time bothering about her husband: "Let not my lord, I pray thee, regard this man of Belial, even Nabal: for as his name is, so is he; Nabal is his name, and folly is with him" (v. 25). She knew him well; and in modern vernacular, her words might have been something like, "Nabal is his name, and stupidity his game!" And then, while respectfully acknowledging David's willingness to fight the Lord's battles and his purity of heart and calling to be king over Israel, she wisely warned that if he were to take this occasion to avenge himself, needlessly shedding the blood of someone who was, after all, his fellow countryman, it would end up being a problem to him, an "offence of heart". Her wisdom won the day as David relented and listened to her advice, sensibly recognising it to be from God.

Nabal subsequently had a night of debauched dining and drinking, "like the feast of a king", and "his heart was merry within him". Abigail—again with wisdom—waited till the next morning, after he had gained some sobriety, to reveal to him her discussion with David, whereupon "his heart died within him, and he became as a stone". About ten days later, he died. "The

LORD smote Nabal" (vv. 36-38). Upon hearing this, David declared, "Blessed be the LORD, that hath pleaded the cause of my reproach from the hand of Nabal, and hath kept his servant from evil: for the LORD hath returned the wickedness of Nabal upon his own head" (v. 39).

Obviously impressed with Abigail, David made plans to marry her. He had learned a lesson that God would take care of matters in His own time. In fact, he had seen "the reward of the wicked".

Occasional rare extremes are still expressed in the Psalms, as in the tragic cry of the exiles in Babylon in Psalm 137. Traumatised and estranged from the God they once knew, seemingly with no grace from Him in their distant place of enslavement and grief, their rage, bitterness, and unjustifiable curses revealed their remorse over the fact that the God they used to be in favour with was now simply a memory. Their imprecations exposed the result of their tragic separation from Him and could not be used to uphold an argument for "retributive" prayer. Out of favour with God, their final vengeful cry inexcusably issued forth from mouths unable to "sing the LORD's song in a strange land". Despite His temporary abandonment, He *could* have helped them had they turned to Him in repentance. Some, however, still see this passage as *hyperbolic* of just retribution on those who despise God and abuse His people.

The New Testament speaks in different ways of the "reward of the wicked" and of those who cause the righteous to suffer. Second Thessalonians chapter one discusses this "righteous judgement of God" (v. 5):

> Seeing it is a righteous thing with God to recompense tribulation to them that trouble you; And to you who are troubled rest with us, when the Lord Jesus shall be revealed from heaven with his mighty angels, In flaming fire taking vengeance on them that know not God, and that obey not the gospel of our Lord Jesus Christ; Who shall be punished with everlasting destruction from the presence of the Lord, and from the glory of his power; When he shall come to be glorified in his saints. (v. 6-10)

The loving Lord and Prince of Peace is referred to here as recompensing tribulation on behalf of His people, in opposition to those who oppress and persecute them ("them that trouble you") and on "them that know not God, and that obey not the gospel". Here is that "rod of iron" we read about in Psalm 2. We have heard of the "great tribulation"—but here it is repayment *with* tribulation. "Recompense" can mean a repayment or requisition for a worthy *or* an unworthy reason. At Jesus' command, the angels will be the agents of judgement at the end of the world (Matt. 13:40-42, 49, 50; 25:31), and Hebrews 10:27 speaks of "a certain fearful looking for of judgement and fiery indignation, which shall devour the adversaries". God alone has entitlement to do this, as seen in Deut. 32:35: "To me belongeth vengeance, and recompense", reiterated in Hebrews 10:30, "vengeance belongeth unto me, I will recompense".

Legitimate and fair retribution *does* sometimes come from those He has rightfully appointed—Jesus' driving out the moneychangers from the temple being an example. God loves all His creation, but action needed to be taken. And with the moneychangers, that meant reasonable, Divine justice. A law-enforcer in a fair society is one who "beareth not the sword in vain" (Rom. 13:4), never to be done out of cruelty and hatred but out of duty and obedience to God's laws and in detestation of their violation. They represent God in this position. To those who do evil, they are "the minister of God, a revenger to execute wrath upon him that doeth evil" (Rom. 13:4). For all those who need to be safe from evildoers, this could be considered to be love in action. Note, however, that this system *rewards* those who are good and *punishes* those who are evil, not the other way around. If the order gets reversed, it becomes authority to be resisted—and this firstly in the spiritual realm—for when tyrants rule, believers' prayers change accordingly. We are instructed to pray for our enemies, but there is the question of *what* to pray. It may be right when tyrants rule to pray that they be changed in heart *or*, conversely, *removed* from their office if they prove consistently unworthy of it—or perhaps both.

Topics such as this are not easy to unpack. Theology has been called a science; but sometimes, it could also be described as the difficult art of trying to think straight on matters related to God or as a school where the student and the teacher sometimes swop seats and where both are lifelong learners.

Read the following passage aloud slowly:

> God is jealous, and the LORD revengeth; the LORD revengeth, and is furious; the LORD will take vengeance on his adversaries, and he reserveth wrath for his enemies. The LORD is slow to anger, and great in power, and will not at all acquit the wicked . . . his fury is poured out like fire . . . The LORD is good, a strong hold in the day of trouble; and he knoweth them that trust in him. (Nahum 1:2, 3a, 6, 7).

The language here in the King James Version includes the reversal (chiasmus) in the first line, the rhyming of "revenge" and "vengeance", the assonance of "acquit" and "wicked", the alliteration of "fury" and "fire", the alliteration and assonance of "trouble" and "trust", a simile ("like fire"), and a metaphor ("a strong hold"). Some people try to avoid such verses, but that is not an option if we believe in the plenary inspired Word of God. We have to take the verses as real and relevant, in their context, even though we may be only starting to grasp some of it.

In Psalm 94:1-6, the unknown psalmist *asks* for it to happen:

1. O LORD God, to whom vengeance belongeth; O God, to whom vengeance belongeth, shew thyself.
2. Lift up thyself, thou judge of the earth; render a reward to the proud.
3. LORD, how long shall the wicked, how long shall the wicked triumph?
4. How long shall they utter and speak hard things? And all the workers of iniquity boast themselves?
5. They break in pieces thy people, O LORD, and afflict thine heritage.
6. They slay the widow and the stranger, and murder the fatherless.

"Shew thyself", "lift up thyself", "render a reward"—these are his pleas. Try saying this one aloud, too. Of literary interest is the use of purposeful repetition, especially in verses one and three.

The psalmist later asks of God a key question, reminiscent again of Psalm 2: "Shall the throne of iniquity have fellowship with thee, which frameth mischief by a law?" (v. 20). He then continues, "They gather themselves together against the soul of the righteous, and condemn the innocent blood. But the LORD is my defence; and my God is the rock of my refuge. And he shall bring upon them their own iniquity, and shall cut them off in their own wickedness; yea, the LORD our God shall cut them off." (Psalm 94:21-23)

If, again, you read this aloud slowly, you will discover the use of alliteration, assonance, and repetition. While the Psalms speak about how "the workers of iniquity . . . break in pieces thy people, O LORD, and afflict thine heritage" (Psalm 94:4-5), when we look at the Bible's final book, we hear "the souls of them that were slain for the word of God, and for the testimony which they held" crying loudly, "How long, O Lord, holy and true, dost thou not judge and avenge our blood on them that dwell on the earth?" (Rev. 6:9-10; see Gen. 4:10), a question and a plea for God's intervention. Here are, or were, saints praying for action on earth about a situation. Should not we who are still on the earth do the same?

Jesus narrated a remarkable parable in Luke 18:1-8. In the first four verses of the preceding chapter, He had given instructions regarding some vital aspects of human relationships concerning offenses and forgiveness. The parable in chapter eighteen speaks of persistence in prayer. A widow importunately approaches someone who in a contradiction of terms is said to be an "unjust judge" (i.e., judges are generally expected to be just). He does not listen to her, but she doggedly perseveres until in exasperation, he grants her request, namely to "avenge me of mine adversary". God is then compared to this unjust judge because He—the truly fair and impartial One—whilst also delaying for His own reasons yet is far more willing than the earthly judge to grant the requests of those who come to Him with persevering faith.

The irony is that just as the unjust judge needed nagging, so God is calling here for "prayerful pestering" until He moves. While He sees the whole story, He is willing to wait till the petitioner is prepared. "The teacher arrives when the student is ready", as the saying goes. After bearing with them awhile and after they have proved themselves to have persistent faith, crying day and night to Him, He eventually avenges—speedily. This parable is pertinent to the discussion under this strophe because the word repeated in Luke (and in Romans 12:19 and again in Revelation 6:10 and 19:2) is "avenge",[94] referring not to revenge but to what comes from due process, from the fair vindication of someone's rights.

The prophets of ancient Israel knew all about this, which is why Jeremiah, for instance, wrote, "Call unto me, and I will answer thee, and shew thee great and mighty things, which thou knowest not" (Jer. 33:3).

The mystery of God's amazing intervention at appropriate times is awe-inspiring since it can be for blessing or judgment, or both at the same time—vindication and preservation for some and fearful verdicts for others.

Sometimes in the Bible, God's "emotions" and actions resist easy explanation, as in Genesis 6:5-6: "God saw that the wickedness of man was great in the earth, and that every imagination of the thoughts of his heart was only evil continually. And it repented the LORD that he had made man on the earth, and it grieved him at his heart". (Verse eleven reveals that "the earth also was corrupt before God, and the earth was filled with violence.") We cannot imagine these "sentiments" of God because we are, again, limited by language. But we know, in small measure, what they are like because, to a degree, we have experienced them ourselves. We have sensed a fraction of His feelings, for He Who is beyond us also communicates them to us. An impersonal force, a power that is not a "person", could not do that. The result was the worldwide flood.

---

94 Vine, 82.

Another psalm along these lines is Psalm 40, which begins with a joyful narrative of the five-fold wonders God had done in David's life after hearing his cry. He had brought him out of a "horrible pit", out of the "miry clay", "set his feet upon a rock", "established his goings", and "put a new song in his mouth"—all from prayer. The second part of verse three states that this would be a testimony and a witness to many, which it has been. In verse four, the beatitude, "Blessed is that man that maketh the LORD his trust, and respecteth not the proud, nor such as turn aside to lies", reminds us that we have no obligation to respect the proud. The *expression* of God's love can be contingent upon the recipient's attitude. One may feel compassion and sympathy for someone; but if that individual is too proud to receive it, is totally given over to evil, or proves himself unreachable and continues to sin despite the grace of God, then life will not go well for him at the end. Eternal love is unfathomable, but it cannot be taken for granted.

Psalm 40 continues as a prayer. David exalts Who God is and praises Him for His wonderful works, for His many thoughts toward us which "cannot be reckoned up in order". Then, he rehearses how doing God's will and having His law in our heart is more to be desired than sacrifice and offering. He reminds God how he had preached righteousness, not held back from speaking, had declared God's faithfulness and salvation, and had revealed God's loving-kindness and truth. Then come the petitions such as, "Withhold not thou thy tender mercies from me, O LORD: let thy lovingkindness and thy truth continually preserve me" (v. 11)—and other requests for deliverance and help. He reminds God of the evils round about, plus his own iniquities, and then states, "Let them be ashamed and confounded together that seek after my soul to destroy it; let them be driven backward and put to shame that wish me evil. Let them be desolate for a reward of their shame that say unto me, Aha, aha" (vv. 14-15).

How many times is the word "shame" used here?

- "Let them be ashamed"
- "Let them be . . . put to shame"
- "A reward of their shame".

What then is the "reward of the wicked"? David knew it. He overcame the evil giant, Goliath—a defeat that brought shame to the proud Philistines; but sadly, he also saw shame come to King Saul and, even more tragically, to his own wayward son Absalom. He had a taste of it in his own life, too, when he went astray.

The "reward" was certainly there in Psalm 40:15—one word: "desolate". "Let them be desolate." According to the Hebrew[95], David is here asking God to "let them be stunned, stupefied, devastated, destroyed, made waste and put to *shame*. Let them be ruined!" The "reward of the wicked" is simply desolation and shame. While David made these supplications, he also had the capacity to forgive and knew from experience that shame *can* bring change, so he finishes by expressing a desire that all those who seek God would be able to rejoice and be full of praise. And in Psalm 43:1, he further implores God for deliverance *from* the wicked: "Judge me, O God, and plead my cause against an ungodly nation: O deliver me from the deceitful and unjust man."

Finally, from the Old Testament is Nehemiah's prayer, made in the face of the determined opposition to his rebuilding of Jerusalem's walls: "Hear, O our God; for we are despised: and turn their reproach upon their own head, and give them for a prey in the land of captivity: And cover not their iniquity, and let not their sin be blotted out from before thee: for they have provoked thee to anger before the builders" (Neh. 4:4-5; cf. Ezek. 11:21). The result of this prayer and Nehemiah's courage was that God "brought their counsel to nought" (4:15).

So can we pray similarly? Our model is Jesus. His ministry and teachings included commands to "love your enemies, bless them that curse you, do good

---

95   Strong, s.v. "shâmêm," 118.

to them that hate you, and pray for them which despitefully use you, and persecute you" (Matt. 5:44). Read the whole of Proverbs 24, especially verses seventeen to twenty and twenty-eight to twenty-nine. "Rejoice not when thine enemy falleth, and let not thine heart be glad when he stumbleth" (v. 17). "Say not, I will do so to him as he hath done to me" (29). Paul wrote, "Bless them which persecute you; bless, and curse not" (Rom. 12:14). He also wrote, "Avenge not yourselves, but rather give place unto wrath, for it is written, Vengeance is mine; I will repay, saith the Lord. Therefore, if thine enemy hunger, feed him; if he thirst, give him drink: for in so doing thou shalt heap coals of fire upon his head. Be not overcome of evil, but overcome evil with good" (Rom. 12:19-21).

The Greek in these verses for "bless" is *ĕulŏgĕō*[96]—to speak well of, to bless, praise, thank or invoke a benediction upon. We are to *eulogise* and give benedictions to (i.e., bless) our enemies. Retribution is not our right, for how then could the blessings of Psalm 91 come? But our enemies *will* come to shame and will *remain* in shame if they never repent.

In Psalm 44, the writer extols God for all His righteous works done in the past towards the nation, then suddenly changes tack and talks about how God had cast the nation off and put them to shame, making them a reproach to their neighbours and their name a "byword among the heathen" (v. 14). Then he reminds God that they had not forgotten Him, and their heart had not turned back from Him; but if they had, then God would know about it because He knows all "the secrets of the heart" (v. 21). Again, shame can bring change.

The writer states, "Yea, for thy sake are we killed all the day long; we are counted as sheep for the slaughter" (Psalm 44:22), a phrase reiterated by Paul near the end of his chapter on the heroes of faith in Romans 8, where he integrates it into his narrative about our security in Christ's love. "Who shall separate us from the love of Christ? shall tribulation, or distress, or persecution, or famine, or nakedness, or peril, or sword? As it is written, For thy sake we are killed all the day long; we are accounted as sheep for the

---

96 Strong, s.v. "ĕulŏgĕō," 33.

slaughter. Nay, in all these things we are more than conquerors through him that loved us" (Rom. 8:35-37).

In Psalm 44:23-26, the unknown writer also pleads with God in a manner reminiscent of the Revelation 6:10 passage: "Awake, why sleepest thou, O Lord? arise, cast us not off for ever. Wherefore hidest thou thy face, and forgettest our affliction and our oppression? For our soul is bowed down to the dust: our belly cleaveth unto the earth. Arise for our help, and redeem us for thy mercies' sake."

Why are you sleeping? Why do you hide your face? Get up and save us! Such phrases sound to us almost cheeky. But are they?

One day, all our bodies will be dust; and our souls will be in eternity. In the meantime, the fact that God sometimes does not seem to show up when we want Him to does not mean He is not interested. And when we see injustice and unmitigated evil against the innocent and the weak, then the call of some of these psalms for evildoers to be put to shame, to be caught in the net they set for others, to fall by their own counsels, to be brought to confusion, to have their speech confused (Psalm 55:9), to have their own mischief come upon their own head, and to be brought low so that all who are oppressed may be lifted up and their afflictions relieved and their souls vindicated can legitimately be part of our prayers too.

And in those prayers, we should not forget to ask God to "in wrath remember mercy" (Hab. 3:2). In the context of the welfare of others affected by evil, however, the requests are valid. And God will answer. Ultimately, we are facing the demonic hordes of evil behind the actions, which I will expand on when we come to verse thirteen. Those who have given in to such evil powers may be made aware of the consequences of their choices by the conviction of the Spirit of God as He calls them to repentance and salvation as a result of our prayers.

In Romans 11:9, considered above under verse three, quoting from David in Psalm 69 we read, "Let their table be made a snare, and a trap, and a stumblingblock, and a recompense unto them: Let their eyes be darkened, that they may not see, and bow down their back always." The apostle Paul is speaking here of the "spirit of slumber" that God allowed to come upon Israel. Due to their apostasy, the Gospel's privileges were denied them. Indeed, David may not have known he was praying such a strategic prayer. Psalm 69 is, in fact, Messianic:

- "They that hate me without a cause" (v. 4)
- "For the zeal of thine house hath eaten me up" (v. 9)
- "In my thirst they gave me vinegar to drink" (v. 21).

The apparent paradoxes of this subject can be deciphered with thought and study. Our spiritual enemies *can* be driven back through prayer. The proud being brought low reveals that God cannot be mocked (Gal. 6:7); but also, He "will have all men to be saved, and to come unto the knowledge of the truth" (I Tim. 2:4). And His enemies' shame can lead them to salvation.

To return once again to the treasure trove of the Psalms, another clue to this question of "reward" is found in Psalm 54:5a: "He shall reward evil unto mine enemies." "Reward" may not only be a euphemism for punishment, for the word translated "reward" in Psalm 54 and in Hosea 4:9 has the sense of returning or causing something to return.[97] Indicating consequences, this could conceivably read, "He shall turn back evil upon mine enemies"—that is, the evil that they do or think will return back upon them. The gist, then, is clearly not only desolation but also that the evil done will be turned back onto themselves. God does not cause evil. Evil and God are diametrically opposed to each other so cannot coexist. They are not two sides of the same coin or occurring on the same continuum or wavelength. (Isaiah 45:7 in this connection requires careful interpreting.[98])

---

97   Strong, s.v. "shûwb," 113.
98   See the collection of comments on it in John W. Halley, *Alleged Discrepancies of the Bible* (Whitaker House, Springdale, PA, n.d.).

But God can arrange for evil to happen by *allowing* it for purposes of judgement, or redemption, or both, in a process with the potential to turn shame into change—although that does not always happen.

Paul's dealings with several spiteful characters in the early church exemplify this, as recorded in I Timothy 1:20, II Timothy 2:17, and II Timothy 4:14. The individuals in question were Hymenaeus, Philetus, and Alexander the coppersmith. Amongst Paul's closing statements in I Corinthians is, "If any man love not the Lord Jesus Christ, let him be Anathema Maranatha" (16:22), the last two words meaning "accursed when the Lord comes".

The Church takes Paul's writings to be Scripture and therefore inspired by the Holy Spirit. He was discussing church matters and encouraging the local believers within that assembly. The standard was to love the Lord Jesus Christ. To "love not" was not referring primarily to a nominal believer yet to discover faith, but to those in the fellowship who were bereft of love towards God, the outgrowth of which would be a lack of love towards His followers. And Alexander was one of those. In speaking of him, Paul employed the word "reward" in II Timothy 4:14: "Alexander the coppersmith did me much evil: the Lord reward him according to his works." Some, such as Paul's critics, may have said that Paul should have loved, forgiven, and prayed for him. We can be confident he would have done so. The time came, however, for decisive action, all else having failed. Paul "delivered [Alexander and Hymenaeus] unto Satan"—and for a specific reason: "that they may learn not to blaspheme" (I Tim. 1:20). They had put away a good conscience and shipwrecked their faith (v. 19).

What Paul meant by delivering or surrendering someone to Satan is uncertain, but implied is that they were *already* yielding themselves to Satan's enticements, putting away a formerly good conscience and in some way blaspheming God. Paul's affectionate prayers had till then kept them from being totally dragged away in spirit and soul into the darkness of the enemy's realm. For how many might this be the case, leaving us unaware when, if ever, to desist in prayer for them? However, in this instance, it seems that Paul did. Some say that Paul was an apostle and thus had a special dispensation to "bind and loose", which we as laity do not have. But he wrote to his followers to follow him as he followed Christ (I Cor. 4:16; 11:1; Phil. 3:17; I Thess. 1:6; II Thess. 3:7). So scripturally, we are enjoined to do as he did and therefore entitled to pray as he prayed. But the purpose even at that point was redemptive and not a relinquishment of responsibility for their souls, for he said that it was so they might "learn not to blaspheme". The capacity to learn from whatever might befall them *may* still have been there at that time and repentance yet possible (see I Cor. 5:5; cf. II Cor. 7:9-10).

Tragically, however, the story does not end well. We read in the final heart-rending mention of Alexander in the second epistle that any possibly redemptive intention in the surrendering of them to Satan had not been successful. The outcome appears to have been the same for Hymenaeus (II Tim. 2:17-18). Paul followed with a final relinquishment of Alexander to God's "reward"—"according to his works". In other words, the evil he did would return upon him, as we saw in some of the Psalms:

> Of whom be thou ware also; for he hath greatly withstood our words. At my first answer no man stood with me, but all men forsook me: I pray God that it may not be laid to their charge. Notwithstanding the Lord stood with me, and strengthened me; that by me the preaching might be fully known, and that all the Gentiles might hear: and I was delivered out of the mouth of the lion. And the Lord shall deliver me from every evil work, and will preserve me unto his heavenly kingdom: to whom be glory for ever and ever. Amen. (II Tim. 4:15-18)

The "mouth of the lion", while possibly a reference to the Christian-eating lions of the arena, could also have been a double entendre, pointing towards the words spoken against the faith and against Paul himself, as he had stated in reference to Hymenaeus and Philetus, "And their word will eat as doth a canker"[99] (II Tim. 2:17). We will see this "lion" again in our study of verse thirteen. What is clear is that the reward of the wicked sometimes coincides with the deliverance of the righteous.

Much of these two Timothy epistles has to do with words, with more than sixty references to both positive and negative speech in them. Paul spoke of Timothy being "nourished up in the words of faith and of good doctrine" (I Tim. 4:6), and Hymenaeus and Alexander had been guilty of blaspheming (i.e., vilifying, speaking impiously, defaming, reviling, speaking evil[100]). This and the statements about pride in the same epistles bring us back again to the Psalms: "For the sin of their mouth and the words of their lips let them even be taken in their pride: and for cursing and lying which they speak" (Psalm 59:12).

A pattern of petitions is here designed to cause those who knowingly and persistently perpetrate evil to stumble and fall at their own sin and for those who commit evil unknowingly to become aware of what they are doing. In both instances, it is also that they may repent and be restored.

And finally, in chapter nineteen of Revelation, the desire of the saints is expressed over the fall of "Babylon", fulfilled in Jesus' return; for "in righteousness he doth judge and make war . . . the armies which were in heaven followed him" (vv. 11, 14). God's vindication is His prerogative, comes in His timing, and is observable.

---

99 Or "gangrene".
100 Strong, s.v. "blasphēmĕō," 19.

CHAPTER 8

PROTECTED FROM EVIL AND PLAGUE

STROPHE THREE (D)

"Because thou hast made the LORD, which is my refuge, even the most High,
thy habitation; There shall no evil befall thee, neither shall any plague come
nigh thy dwelling." (vv. 9-10)

HERE IN THE MIDDLE of the psalm is another key statement:
"Because you have done this, here is the twofold result." Again, typically we
have twos and threes for emphasis: the LORD / the most High; my refuge /
thy habitation / thy dwelling; no evil / neither any plague.

While "my refuge" could also read "thy refuge", the wisdom of the King
James Version translators can be trusted here; and the former reads better, in
my opinion. Whether "my" or "thy" reads better, however, the main focus of
this dependent clause is its key word, "refuge", pointing to the driving causes
for the all-important choice of making God one's habitation. *Yehôvâh*[101] is
speaker two's Refuge—his place of shelter and hope—as in verse two, and the
speaker is the refugee. The word for "habitation" also opens Moses' preceding
prayer: "Our dwelling place in all generations" (Psalm 90:1).

Here once again, as in verse one, is the Hebrew and Aramaic word for the
Most High, derived from a root verb with a variety of meanings but initially

---

101   Strong, s.v. "Yehôvâh," 47.

to ascend or to be high[102]. *'Ēl 'elyôwn*[103] ("the most High God") is used by Abram and Melchizedek in chapter fourteen of Genesis and by the king of Babylon (alias "Lucifer" or Satan) in stating his intention to "be like the most High" (Isa. 14:14). Used elsewhere of the majesty, transcendence, and greatness of God, it occurs seventeen times in the Psalms, including twice here and at the start of Psalm 92, four times in the book of Daniel referring to "the saints of the most High", and nine times there in its Chaldean form, also rendered as "Most High".

So no evil or plague will "befall" you. It will not approach you, meet you, or happen to you. Neither will it come near your place of residence. "Plague" is used here as it is in every instance throughout Exodus and Leviticus, indicating a blow, infliction, spot, plague, sore, stroke, or wound. When Israel disobeyed God, God sent a plague upon them, so it can go the other way, too. "And the LORD plagued the people, because they made the calf, which Aaron made" (Exod. 32:35). For this inexcusable sin, God held both Aaron and the people responsible at the time of the giving of the Decalogue (the Ten Commandments). Read also Numbers 16:46 for a later occurrence. And when some Israelites committed immorality with the Moabites, twenty-four thousand died (Num. 25).

No safe refuge exists outside the Lord God Almighty, for there is no other "Most High" who will have us live with him, including here and now. He is our spiritual Abode, our Habitation, our House, our Home. "Dwelling" is a covering, tabernacle, or tent, as discussed above regarding Psalm 27:5. It is the safest place on the planet; and as we remain with Him in our spiritual home, no evil will occur, wherever we are; it will also not come near our physical lodging, be that temporary or permanent, humble, or luxurious. If evil begins to arise, God will move the believer to a safe place or supernaturally protect him—according to this psalm. Since this is what it states, it places it beyond

---

102 Strong, s.v. "'âlâh," 88.
103 Strong, s.v. "'elyôwn," 88.

personal opinion or interpretation. The old English etymology of the word "evil" has its roots in the concept of exceeding vitally important limits.[104] The Hebrew word for "evil" indicates adversity, affliction, and calamity[105], the opposite of good.

This does not imply absence of persecution, which all the righteous featured in the Bible faced, and from which true believers are not exempt (see Heb. 11). Evil, however, will not touch the soul of the one safe in the secret place, and even the evil inherent *within* persecution can be mitigated by God's hand—if, that is, we are to believe this psalm. For God, in His wisdom, encourages us in the Lord's Prayer to pray that we may be delivered from evil. And perhaps the main reason for this wide-ranging request is that we have so little comprehension of its nature, magnitude, and power. That lack of understanding has been ordained by God because around us is enough to cause us to lose sleep at night were we to be conscious of its full extent. Rather, we need awareness of the love and power of God.

So verses nine and ten have a reason word, "because"; the subject, "you"; the verb, "have made"; two names for God; two spiritual places (refuge and habitation); one physical place (dwelling); and two results of making God our Refuge: no evil, and no plague.

Verse eleven then reads, "For he shall give his angels charge over thee, to keep thee in all thy ways". "For", synonymous with "because", links to verse ten, and here is another means for deliverance from evil and plague—angels. These beings move as God despatches them: God present, angels surrounding, the believer making God his habitation. No evil will befall, nor will any plague come near the believer—not only because the believer has taken the initiative to make the Lord his or her habitation but also because God has taken the initiative to give Divine assistance.

---

104 Hoad, 158.
105 Strong, s.v. "ra'," 109.

"Angels" are messengers or anyone despatched to do a job as a deputy for another; so also could be ambassadors, kings, prophets, priests, or teachers. The reference in this verse is to real angels appointed to be in "charge" over the believer. These beings appear throughout Scripture. They are not occultic spirits, departed souls, hallucinations, fanciful myths, fictitious creatures, or figments of the imagination. And while not necessarily all winged, some are (e.g., seraphim). They are powerful and, though completely different from us, can engage with humans when commissioned by God in their serving capacity as messengers and protectors. They cannot be summoned by us nor prayed to, but God despatches them on special occasions to special people (as in the Christmas story of Mary, Jesus' mother, for example). And they are active today, too, perhaps more often than we think. Angels exist. Sometimes they even appear as normal humans.

When Satan tried to use this verse to tempt Jesus to leap off a pinnacle of the Jerusalem temple, he was clearly referring to a real angel who would supposedly then catch Jesus on the way down. The theory was that Jesus could have thus proved Himself superior to and distinct from others and, in the process, demonstrated for all time that angels were a reality. Had "angels" been only a reference to prophets or priests, it would have been meaningless. Characteristically, though, Satan misquoted the verse. So in the Matthew narration, "to keep thee in all thy ways" is missing; and in Luke's, "in all thy ways" is missing. These are unlikely to be scribal errors, despite the New Testament's use of the Septuagint (Greek translation of the Old Testament), especially in Matthew. The phrase "to keep thee in all thy ways" is a necessary part of the equation; "the steps of a good man are ordered by the Lord" (Psalm 37:23), Who "knoweth the way of the righteous" (Psalm 1:6). This incident provided a disincentive to any deviation from that way; for when our ways are God's ways, we will not be easy targets for Satan to entice to "test" or "prove" God.

Keeping us safe and guarding and protecting us is part of what angels do. Here and in the next two verses, the believer is not hiding away in retreat, nor even in his own dwelling necessarily, but out where his "ways" take him through stony territory, where lions, adders, and dragons are—in the world but, in his heart, not of it.

Following is a testimony of what this all means in practical terms. It comes from my wife's experience as a youngster of about eleven years of age. (She has been a believer in Jesus since she was around five.)

One day, she asked her father if she could visit some of her cousins in another city, the capital of her country. This was a several hours' drive north of her hometown on roads that wound up through rugged terrain beside rivers cascading down from the Himalayan mountains.

Her father had sent her away with a close friend of his, who commuted regularly between the two cities. The next day, when it was time for her to go home, he arranged for her to fit into the back of a four-wheel drive with others going the same route. As they prepared to leave for the journey down the twisting roads, she suddenly sensed something strange, a feeling of alarm that made her jump out of the vehicle and run back down the road towards the bus station. Her father's friend chased after her. Though he tried his best, she flatly refused to return to the vehicle. Furious, he found a bus for her; and together, they began the journey back.

After about an hour, the bus turned a corner; and a horrific scene confronted them. A jeep had gone off the road. One man, who had been catapulted out of the vehicle, lay at the side of the road, gasping for breath. He was dying. Another had saved himself by jumping out at the last minute. The jeep and all its other occupants had plunged down a ravine, disappearing deep into the depths of the rushing mountain river far below. It was the same vehicle that she had run away from!

The man who had accompanied her in the bus was astounded.

"How did you know?" he asked.

Her desperate father arrived at the scene and, overwhelmed with emotion and relief, saw his daughter standing there safe and sound. What, or Who, had warned her? Was it the Holy Spirit or an angel?

Here, we need to be reminded that Psalm 91 deals primarily with the big issues: plagues, terrors, destructions, lions, snakes, and dragons. "They shall bear thee up in their hands, lest thou dash thy foot against a stone." (v. 12) Yet in the midst of all these hazards and upheavals, small matters are important, too—*and* the not-so-small, as you will know if you have ever twisted your foot or tripped on a steep pathway. So while the phrase may imply more than simply tripping up, whether serious or seemingly insignificant, the caring, protecting angels are there. Also, the path is not always smooth. We *will* face obstacles. Sometimes, God protects us or minimises the impact; while at other times, we have to learn to tread more carefully. As we walk in His ways, however, He teaches us to move more accurately and in His Divine timing and to learn the habit of prayer beforehand so that we make fewer mistakes.

So while "bear thee up" can be literally fulfilled, it can be metaphorical, too. And "dash thy foot against a stone" can refer to unintentional mistakes and misjudgements, including those potentially harmful to our spiritual, mental, emotional, physical, or relational health.

The first part of the statement (beginning in verse eleven) is literal, and the second clause completes the couplet of these two mostly monosyllabic verses. The context is of walking, of forward movement, of trudging, climbing, and progressing. Leviticus 26:3 speaks of *walking* in God's statutes as well as *keeping* and *doing* His commandments. Walking is obeying those statutes, doing His will, and loving Him with all our heart, soul, strength, and mind (Luke 10:27), implying *subconscious awareness* just as our bodily movements are subconscious once we choose to walk in a certain direction. But in the case of His commandments, prior familiarity is a prerequisite. Keeping implies *conscious* obedience. Doing is *acting on* the commandments.

So verses eleven and twelve plainly mean protection from misfortune. "Dash" here (and only here) means to push, gore, defeat, stub a toe, inflict a disease, plague, smite, strike, stumble, and put to the worse.[106] While we all may stub a toe occasionally, we are taught here that *all* potential danger is known by God and often, it would seem, by His angels. A full guarantee this may not be, though, because at all times, we must remember the intent of the psalm in which we are enjoined to live in the secret place of the Most High "from Whom all blessings flow".[107] To do that, we must take Him at His word.

The whole counsel of God implies that not all afflictions will inevitably or immediately disappear ("Many are the afflictions of the righteous", Psalm 34:19a), but deliverance is available ("the LORD delivereth him out of them all", Psalm 34:19b). The tenor of Scripture states that though God may not always take away potential dangers, He nevertheless can protect us *from* them or prevent our being irreparably damaged while going *through* them. He has all authority, and angels are clearly revealed as part of His solution.

I had a serious accident in my younger years, and, like most of us, have had a few serious sicknesses. In the former, I believe, not coincidentally, I had not been circumspect about my choice of friends at the time; and perhaps that had somewhat to do with it. Yet how can we be certain that at *any* period in our life all will go smoothly? How can we know what is around the corner? Naturally, we cannot. But again, this psalm does give certain assurances to those who are willing to apply it and trust in its message. We *can* believe it and the God Who inspired it and speaks in and through it. His words are true. No hidden messages, secret codes, or undisclosed mysteries are there. A child may read, believe, understand, and live by this psalm; and to them, God will

---

106 Strong, s.v. "nâgaph," 76.
107 Thomas Ken, "Praise God From Whom All Blessings Flow," *Melodies of Praise* (Springfield: Gospel Publishing House, 1957), 341, public domain.

be as real and as faithful as to the elderly or anyone else who approaches it with like faith.

As with any part of Scripture, Psalm 91 can be exegeted and understood in more depth, as I have been at pains to do here. And in both its simplicities and complexities, it can lead us towards a walk with God with a confidence and assurance we may never have known before. We must first try it, believe it, and trust it. And the more that we know it, the less we can ignore or dismiss it. This is a walk to be learnt.

In each case of difficulty, God graciously teaches us, protecting from worse; and often later, after the events, we can praise Him. God chastens, too, for we are His children and He our Father. And in the early days, as we grow, He deals firmly but also gently—ameliorating, advising, comforting, counselling, helping, informing us of better ways, promising a better future— and healing. As the hymn goes, "Earth has no sorrow that heaven cannot heal".[108] Sometimes, too, this means physical healing.

God's warnings and guidance are also part of the process of His protection. If consequences of past decisions remain; then in "the valley of the shadow of death", we "fear no evil" (Psalm 23:4). The right medical care may save us, or God Himself, especially when there are no other means. I am personally grateful for some small but significant Divine healings. His provision at times also comes through "normal" means, God also providing His peace, assurance, and special touch.

Not only that, but all of us have had near misses, too—probably many that we do not know about and never will—yet God was there. Angels, as His humble servants, seldom give awareness of their presence. If they do, then that is an occasion for praise to God. They are available for whenever God needs them for His people and His Church. While their involvement is rarely revealed in personal, ecclesiastical, or national affairs, we have the assurance

---

108 Thomas Moore, "Come, Ye Disconsolate" (1046 Hymnals), https://hymnary.org/text/
come_ye_disconsolate_whereer_ye_languish, public domain.

that they are constantly before God's face, worshipping Him and ready to do His bidding at a moment's notice. Psalm 103:20 states, "Bless the LORD, ye his angels, that excel in strength, that do his commandments, hearkening unto the voice of his word." (Refer also to Revelation 5:11-12).

Of course, "charge over thee" could include "talk to you", "tell you what to do", or "guide you". However, although none of those are beyond their ability or role, we are never instructed to appeal to angels or attempt to invoke their attention. As believers, we have God's Holy Spirit and His Word to guide us, both sufficient as our primary sources of inspiration and information. Along with these, wise counsel from others is advisable. While we must not approach God presumptively, His communications through the Bible and the help He provides from prudent people can protect against any evil that tries to beset us.

We must look after ourselves, exercise, get good nutrition, and simply pray that His "will be done in earth, as it is in heaven", that He would "lead us not into temptation" or trial "but deliver us from evil" (Matt. 6:10, 13). Again, His angels are there; and on His prompting and under His jurisdiction, they *will* keep us in all our ways. We need not question these verses. And if it has not happened so far, then perhaps with this fresh understanding, now is the time.

Whether wise advice, the Holy Spirit, the Word, or angels, God has resources to help us throughout our lives. We can have confidence that these wonderful beings, 100 percent loyal to God, are, by His grace, given charge over His people in ways we may never fully understand. What an encouragement and comfort to know. The contrast in this verse, then, is hands and feet—the angels' hands and our feet. God guides. Angels guard. We walk.

CHAPTER 9

LIONS, ADDERS, AND THE DRAGON

STROPHE THREE (E)

"Thou shalt tread upon the lion and adder: the young lion and the dragon
shalt thou trample under feet." (v. 13)

FEET ARE A FEATURE theme, a motif, of these verses twelve and thirteen. From being protected from dashing our foot against a stone to having a wonderful backing of friendly forces as depicted in the previous two verses, we can now triumphantly trample over our spiritual foes.

Here again is a chiasmus—"Thou shalt tread . . . shalt thou trample"—the grammatical structure reversed in the restatement. This comes again in the next verse. The verbs, comparable in meaning, start with the same consonant /tr/. Here is emphatic synonymous parallelism, a double with both subtle and noticeable differences, repetition purposefully enhancing the literary appeal with the nuances supporting the couplet's structure. People do not speak like this; it is poetic.

This verse completes this longest strophe of the psalm, picturing the total triumph of the one addressed as "thou/thee" over his archenemies. It shows assertive action—*our* action. But treading upon lions and adders, young lions and dragons could only ever be figurative, and so other passages can be brought in to assist us with clues about the meaning of the verse in its place in the psalm's message of triumph over adversity. Answers are to be found in two areas: first in any references to lions, adders, young lions, and dragons in the Psalms and in the Bible as a whole and second in this verse's two verbs, "tread" and "trample".

Both words for "lion", while different, refer to the same animal. The first occurrence derives from the root "to roar". "Adder" is *pethen*.[109] Our word "python" comes from the Greek *pûthōn*, a serpent killed by Apollo in Greek mythology[110]; but in old English, it could mean any serpent. The dragon could be either a marine or land monster. Although another meaning given is "jackal" (as in Malachi 1:3, Isaiah 34:13, and in Jeremiah—except 51:34, where it could not possibly be referring to a jackal), the usual context implies a much larger beast, such as a sea serpent, whale, or even a dinosaur.[111] Either way, this monster, the last in the list, is the largest, the most ferocious, and the most dangerous. We may as well say that "dragon" is hyperbolic for the worst enemy you could imagine. The list of these animals links with the previous verses, the connection being the theme of the feet and the step (our walk), the contrast being the fact that while in verses eleven and twelve, angels lift us up in case we trip over a rock, here we *intentionally* tread on dangerous predators.

Although accidentally stepping on a real snake is possible in some parts of the world (as it was on Melita where Paul was accidentally bitten by a snake yet protected by God, as described in Acts 28:1-6), no one in their right mind knowingly steps on a snake or lion. Clearly representational then, this metaphor is reiterated in the New Testament where, for instance, Paul was "delivered out of the mouth of the lion" (II Tim. 4:17)—the lion possibly being Paul's persecutors or the one Peter warned us to watch out for when he wrote of our foe who walks about like a "roaring lion . . . seeking whom he may devour" (i.e., the devil—I Peter 5:8).

---

109 Strong, s.v. "pethen," 98.
110 Hoad, "pûthōn," 380.
111 "Dinosaur Questions and Answers." CREATION.com, 1 August 2018, https://creation.com/dinosaur-questions-and-answers.

Other instances of the use of these words in the psalter include:

- Psalm 7:1, where David prays that God would save him from all those who persecuted him, "lest he tear my soul like a lion, rending it in pieces, while there is none to deliver" (v. 2)
- Psalm 10:9, where he speaks of the wicked who persecutes the poor as one who lies "in wait secretly as a lion in his den"
- Psalm 17:9, where he refers to the wicked "that oppress me . . . my deadly enemies, who compass me about" that they are "like as a lion that is greedy of his prey, and as it were a young lion, lurking in secret places" (v. 12).

We read of "like a lion" and "like young lions" in Isaiah, with militaristic overtones as God says of Israel's enemies—the nations—that He would summon them to come quickly as a judgement upon His people (Isa. 5:26-30). And the kings of Assyria and Babylon are called lions in Jeremiah 50:17, 44. Two words are used for lion in Psalm 91, the second translated as "young lion" (as also in Psalm 17:12) [112] [113] [114].

Most of the latter examples were similes (i.e., *like* a lion). But in Psalm 57:4, we see four metaphors: "My soul is among lions: and I lie even among them that are set on fire, even the sons of men, whose teeth are spears and arrows, and their tongue a sharp sword."

David desires an unusual consequence for "the wicked" that were annoying him. In Psalm 58:6, he asks God to "break their teeth . . . in their mouth: break out the great teeth of the young lions, O LORD". In the previous psalm, he used the two images of lions being men whose teeth were "spears and arrows"—symbolic of hateful words. The breaking of the teeth points to God's removing the power of their words and their means of gaining

---

112 Strong, s.v. "shachal," 114.
113 Strong, s.v. "kephîyr," 57.
114 Strong, s.v. "'ârîy," 16.

sustenance. David is lyrical in Psalm 58 in his plea for justice against those who are hardened liars, and violent. We are pointed back to our verse when he says that these people are like snakes: "Their poison is like the poison of a serpent: they are like the deaf adder that stoppeth her ear; which will not hearken to the voice of charmers" (v. 4-5). "Adder" here is the same as in Psalm 91:13. David then gave us clues about who the lion, adder, and young lions are.

We have considered some of the historical context in our study of verses seven and eight, for David's life was reflected chronologically to a degree as his psalms progressed. Psalms 51-60 start with his sad, penitential song (Psalm 51), written after his adultery and murder were exposed, and continue in the context of subsequent challenges he faced from those who resisted his reign, including some from his own family. They contain his prayers, cries for mercy, laments, and moments of praise and rejoicing. Being a "man of war" (I Chron. 28:3), however, he was not permitted to build the temple, for though seeking to love and serve God, he had also "shed blood abundantly, and . . . made great wars". Hence, God stated, "Thou shalt not build an house unto my name, because thou hast shed much blood upon the earth in my sight" (I Chron. 22:8). His son Solomon (whose name meant peaceable or perfect[115]) built the temple instead. "I will give him rest from all his enemies round about: for his name shall be Solomon and I will give peace and quietness unto Israel in his days" (v. 9).

While we must see the psalms of David in light of all this, undiminished is the fact that the Holy Spirit inspired his psalms. So Acts 2:30 reminds us that he was "a prophet". The authorship of Books III and IV is mixed: Asaph, Moses, Solomon, the sons of Korah, David, and anonymous authors. I mentioned earlier that the authorship of Psalm 91 would not seem as important as its Divine inspiration, since if we knew who wrote it then we might be always looking for historical context. But no definitive context can be found. So while the psalmist was inspired by God—with God appearing personally in

---

115   Strong, s.v. "shelômôh," 117.

the last three verses—we still need to look elsewhere for background to a passage such as this.

So what are the clues David gave to help us with this verse? If Psalm 91 is a direct reference—albeit in figurative language—to our flesh and blood enemies and persecutors, are we, in reality, meant to tread upon them, trample over them, and stamp them down, even though God said He would do that to *His* enemies (Isa. 63:3-6)?

And what about the dragon, for an answer to that may give hints to help answer the previous questions? In the Old Testament, no clear picture presents itself as to what a dragon was, except a strong and large animal of some kind. It could be on land or sea. Psalm 74:13-14 states, "Thou didst divide the sea by thy strength: thou brakest the heads of the dragons in the waters. Thou brakest the heads of leviathan in pieces." Leviathan, mentioned five times in the Old Testament, and the dragon, occur together several times. Leviathan is symbolic of Pharaoh in Psalm 74, and the "dragons" are symbolic of the whole Egyptian army. God divided the Red Sea, which closed in again upon the Egyptians after Israel had crossed. Similarly, in Ezekiel 29:3, we read, "Behold I am against thee, Pharaoh king of Egypt, the great dragon that lieth in the midst of his rivers." Pharaoh himself here is a "great dragon".

The dragon is also mentioned in Isaiah 27:1, along with leviathan (a "piercing serpent" and a "crooked serpent"), whom God says He will punish: "In that day the LORD with his sore and great and strong sword shall punish leviathan the piercing serpent, even leviathan that crooked serpent; and he shall slay the dragon that is in the sea." Since the sea can be symbolic of people, who is the dragon in the sea? And who, in turn, is "Pharaoh"? Could leviathan *and* the dragon be synonyms for powers that operate *in the spirit* of Pharaoh?

For in Isaiah 51:9-16, again the connection between the dragon and Rahab, figurative of Egypt, appears, closely connected again with leviathan. Rahab[116]

---

116 Strong, s.v. "râchâb," 108.

in legend was a "female monster of chaos".[117] Verse nine states, "Art thou not it that hath cut Rahab, and wounded the dragon?"

Who, then, is God punishing here in all these instances? Surely not an animal, for animals are not personal enemies of people or of God; but the New Testament sheds light on the whole picture in the book of Revelation's thirteen references to "dragon". Revelation 12:3 says, "And there appeared another wonder in heaven; and behold a great red dragon, having seven heads and ten horns, and seven crowns upon his heads". We also read in Revelation 20:2, "And he laid hold on the dragon, that old serpent, which is the Devil, and Satan".

The word "dragon" traced through, like "lion" and "young lion", is a reference to the enemies of Israel (the Egyptians and Pharaoh) and is symbolic of pride and of Satan, the spirit behind the pharaoh of Moses' day historically seeking to persecute God's people up to and including today. The book of Revelation has stated his identity plainly and speaks of his demise (Rev. 20:2).

The strophe finishes with "the dragon shalt thou trample under feet". The triumph is in the trampling—and that on the most powerful of the four predators mentioned, which in its New Testament meaning and in folklore is far more powerful than a lion or adder. We recall Jesus' words in Luke 10:18-19: "I beheld Satan as lightning fall from heaven. Behold, I give unto you power to tread on serpents and scorpions, and over all the power of the enemy: and nothing shall by any means hurt you." The animals mentioned in verse thirteen of Psalm 91 are, of course, not real, although a literal reading in a few instances could be applied, such as David and Samson triumphing over real lions and Paul over the Melitan snake. Instead, however, they symbolise people, and yet only in the first instance; for while David's descriptions in other psalms of the lions and adders are clearly symbolic of wicked persecutors and oppressors, behind them is the "dragon" himself.

Although we are instructed in the New Testament to love, forgive, bless, and pray for persecutors and oppressors, as confirmed by Old Testament

---

117   J.D. Douglas, *The New Bible Dictionary* (Leicester, England: Inter-Varsity Press, 1978), 1074.

references, these animals further represent the spiritual powers behind those persecuting people, *plus* the dragon—Satan. Insomuch as individuals give themselves completely over to these forces, praying that their scheming, plotting, lying, and oppressing would be exposed and come to nought, that they would "fall by their own counsels . . . for they have rebelled against thee" (Psalm 5:10) is legitimate—prayer not only for our benefit but also on behalf of those affected by oppression. We may pray "against" an enemy (paradoxically also "eulogising" them, as we saw earlier) because we know that the issue is what is behind them. "LORD, thou hast heard the desire of the humble: thou wilt prepare their heart, thou wilt cause thine ear to hear: To judge the fatherless and the oppressed, that the man of the earth may no more oppress [or terrify]" (Psalm 10:17, 18). Much of this has been discussed in detail in the comments on verse eight and in the Psalm 2 commentary.

But let us think about what those people have given themselves over to. In Ephesians 6:12, Paul describes how to do battle: "For we wrestle not against flesh and blood, but against principalities, against powers, against the rulers of the darkness of this world, against spiritual wickedness in high places." Here is the expansion of "tread" and "trample". Picture someone standing in one place treading on and trampling over threats that need to be completely crushed and ground into the dust. Here is the answer: conflict with the powers of darkness as they manifest through circumstances and people and believers treading on invisible powers and stopping the "mouths of lions" (Heb. 11:33). The primary reference in Hebrews was to Gideon, Barak, Samson, Jephthah, David, Samuel, and the prophets, "who through faith subdued kingdoms, wrought righteousness, obtained promises, stopped the mouths of lions" (Heb. 11:33). Samson, David, and Daniel, through their faithfulness to God, literally did this either by killing them or by God's stopping the lions from attacking them, demonstrating the truth in Hebrews 11:1: "Faith is the substance of things hoped for, the evidence of things not seen."

I said earlier that we would be looking at two areas: first, at any relevant references in the Word of God to lions, adders, young lions, and dragons; and second, at the two verbs "tread" and "trample".

God, in His final statements to Job, stated that it was *His* (God's) prerogative to "tread down the wicked" (Job 40:12). Psalms 60:12 and 108:13 read similarly: "Through God we shall do valiantly: for He it is that shall tread down our enemies." We have seen Isaiah 63:1-6 quoting strong sentiments: "I will tread them in mine anger, and trample them in my fury." But in Psalm 44, the writer himself boldly states, "Through thy name will we tread them under that rise up against us" (v. 5). And the closing passage of the Old Testament states that those who fear God's name "shall tread down the wicked: for they shall be ashes under the soles of your feet in the day that I shall do this, saith the LORD of hosts" (Mal. 4:3). That "day" is the time of the coming of the "Sun of righteousness", arising "with healing in his wings" (v. 2), as seen in our verse four study of "wings".

So, while "tread" here refers to the power the Messiah would give those who fear His name, much remains metaphorical (the mention of feet, for instance). To believers is given this task, and the meaning is to be spiritually discerned.

Jesus states who we will be "treading down" in the Great Commission in Mark 16:15-18, expanding on Matthew's version (Matt. 28:18-20): "They shall take up serpents, and if they drink any deadly thing, it shall not hurt them; they shall lay hands on the sick, and they shall recover" (Mark 16:18).

The wording is not "*if* they take up" but "they *shall* take up" (i.e., an expectation). Drinking a "deadly thing", however, has an *if*—"if they drink", so it can only be talking about either an unintentional imbibing of something harmful or an attempted poisoning.

But "take up" cannot possibly mean a deliberate act of handling snakes for show or trying to demonstrate "spirituality", a practice that would prove nothing. The original Koine (everyday Greek of the New Testament) can mean "to take up" but also "to take away, put away, remove"[118]. Hence, it could read, "They shall *remove* serpents", which makes sense because only in the process of removing them would they at all be taking them up. Jesus exhorts His followers to *tread on* serpents (i.e., remove or destroy them). Furthermore, Paul did not "take up" a snake in Acts 28:3; but it latched onto him, whereupon he *removed* it into the fire. Paul's simply shaking it off into the fire proves that God is well able to protect His people from the result of even a literal snake bite.

These truths indicate our spiritual calling, in line with Mark 16:18 and Luke 10, where Jesus commissioned seventy of his followers to go into outlying towns, stay in the houses of welcoming families, speak peace to them, heal any sick, and proclaim that the kingdom of God had come near to them (v. 9). When they returned, they rejoiced because demons were in subjection to them through His name (v. 17), to which He responded, "I beheld Satan as lightning fall from heaven. Behold, I give unto you power to tread on serpents and scorpions, and over all the power of the enemy: and nothing shall by any means hurt you. Notwithstanding in this rejoice not, that the spirits are subject unto you, but rather rejoice, because your names are written in heaven" (Luke 10:18-20).

If this were only for the seventy, would the commission in Matthew 28 and Mark 16 also have been solely for the twelve disciples? And if so, what then of the rest of the New Testament? Clearly, the "serpents", "scorpions", and the "enemy" are "the spirits". So the parts relevant to what we are studying are the following: "I give unto you power to tread on serpents and scorpions, and over all the power of the enemy: and nothing shall by any means hurt you", "the spirits are subject unto you", and "the kingdom of God is come nigh unto you". "Tread on serpents" is virtually verbatim from Psalm 91: "tread upon . . . the adder".

So the "seventy" provided a model in many respects, since we have also been instructed to pray "thy kingdom come" (Matt. 6:10), and this has never

---

118   "G142 - airō - Strong's Greek Lexicon (mgnt)," Blue Letter Bible, Accessed 14 August 2023, https://www.blueletterbible.org/lexicon/g142/mgnt/tr/0-1/.

been rescinded. Also, we are not to be "moved away from the hope of the gospel" (Col. 1:23). The New Testament preaches that the power of this news can bring people to salvation, removing satanic hindrances to their becoming believers in Christ Jesus. And this part of the psalm is what takes place in the private—and sometimes public—place of prayer. The lion, adder, young lion, and dragon represent our spiritual foes.

Lions stealthily hunt their prey and then come suddenly with a terrifying roar, with intensity and power. They stalk, then pounce. Young lions are comparable to the older ones but awkward and lacking in experience, learning, making mistakes, sometimes playing with their prey. As they grow stronger, they may become faster and more daring than the older ones. The only protection is to face them front on with a suitable weapon, the use of which has been learned effectively through training, practice, and real-life scenarios—as Samson and David did in real life. Our approach is to be through the use of the "sword of the Spirit" (Eph. 5:17), the Word of God wielded wisely and effectively, ensuring that they tremble before God's power. And we also have with us "the Lion of the tribe of Judah" (Rev. 5:5).

The word "adder" is now often used for vipers. To illustrate this verse, we could take examples from any serpents. Present-day Israel has forty-two species of snakes, nine being deadly. The common Palestinian viper can grow up to five feet; and the small saw-scaled viper, found in Arabia, Africa, and southwestern Asia, is possibly the most venomous. The more aggressive types of vipers illustrate the kind of enemy that strikes suddenly and without warning, though usually when they feel threatened. Pythons in the long-distant past were native to much of Europe, but the closest to the Middle East now would be in the Sudan. They approach their prey slowly and soundlessly, capturing and gradually constricting it, and often swallowing it whole. This illustrates the enemies who try to constrict and hem us in, seeking to spiritually suffocate and stop believers from moving forward in the right direction and trying to destroy their effectiveness. For this type of serpent, a sharp blade (metaphorically speaking) would provide useful protection—the "two-edged sword" of the Word.

Naturally, the "dragon" is the most obviously beyond our natural ability to resist due to its ferocity and size, but again, God's weapons are on hand. Additionally, we have the help of angels to keep us in all our ways. So we are not alone.

To return to our two verbs then: "tread upon[119]" and "trample[120]" take us to a place of confrontation and conquest. In practice, this might involve a simple, short declaration on our part, such as, "I trample under foot that 'lion' in the name of Jesus", setting the tone of the struggle in our favour. Essentially, it is "walking over" your *spiritual* adversaries. Jesus Himself did, and will do, this. The first of these verbs is mentioned three times in Isaiah 63:2-3 as "treadeth", "trodden", and "tread"; and the second is mentioned once ("trample") (see Hebrews 2:8-9).

These foes are not to be feared; for although their demonic forces will not be fully defeated until death and Hell, "the beast and the false prophet", and Satan are "cast into the lake of fire" (Rev. 20:10, 14), their present-day schemes can be frustrated as they are removed from our way, evicted from our homes, and, by God's grace, put far away from our loved ones and the people and communities we seek to reach (i.e., those who receive us—Luke 10:10; Acts 13:51). Ephesians 6:12 uses the verb "wrestle" in reference to our struggle against the powers of darkness. The sentiment there is the same as Psalm 91:13's "tread upon" and "trample under". No one wrestles to lose—all fighters fight to win. Neither do we expect combat forever, but ultimately— sooner or later—victory.

Earlier in the epistle, Ephesians tells us:

> That ye may know . . . what is the exceeding greatness of his
> power to us-ward who believe, according to the working of his

---

119 Strong, s.v. "dârak," 31.
120 Strong, s.v. "râmaç," 109.

mighty power, Which he wrought in Christ, when he raised him from the dead, and set him at his own right hand in the heavenly places, Far above all principality, and power, and might, and dominion, and every name that is named, not only in this world, but also in that which is to come: And hath put all things under his feet. (Eph. 1:18-22)

Under *His* feet (see I Cor. 15:25, 27; Heb. 2:8). And here is what *our* feet do, too, for if all things are already under *His* feet, then we need not be surprised that some should also come under *ours*. People who have the Most High as their habitation will seek to ensure this; for while the rest of the psalm is about what God will do for those who trustfully abide in Him, here in verse thirteen is the significant action point. Psalm 121:3 echoes that "he will not suffer thy foot to be moved", speaking more about how God's child is kept and preserved. The word used in Psalm 91:11 for "keep" is also used in Psalm 121 for both "keep" and "preserve" (vv. 3, 7-8). And in Psalm 121:5, we read, "The LORD is thy keeper: the LORD is thy shade [the same as "shadow"in 91:1] upon thy right hand".

So not only are we kept from being moved and saved from stumbling—according to Psalm 91:11-13—but we are also told *what* the secret-place-dwellers must do in addition to dwelling. They are to tread over their spiritual adversaries—initially, I believe, through prayer in connection with God and then through declaration. On occasion, I have seen amazing, even instant, changes with situations and people through silent prayer along these lines.

God does not ask us to ask Him to do it. He says, *you* do the treading! It does not work in our own strength but must be in tandem with the Holy Spirit. And in the overall context of prayer, declaration is not a collection of self-gratifying, self-confirming statements but words levelled at a situation with the purpose of changing, pacifying, or reaching out to someone and dealing with any adverse powers affecting them.

The key is the name of Jesus, bringing the kingdom of God to bear on a situation by directing words from God to the contrary powers—not trying to force, debate, or push people a certain way but rather engaging in heavy-duty spiritual combat in the battle gear of an expert fighter. Read again Ephesians 6 regarding the "rulers of the darkness of this world" and "spiritual wickedness in high places" (v. 12). This means being fit, well-drilled, spiritually assertive, unyielding, determined, and willing to adopt it as a lifestyle. It happens in the unseen world around us yet plays itself out in the material world.

The question remains: are we also trampling over Satan? Ultimately, God treads the devil under *our* feet, as Romans 16:20 states: "And the God of peace shall bruise Satan under your feet shortly." "Bruise" here means to tread on, completely crush, shatter, or break in pieces.[121] We know that Satan is the dragon; for in Revelation 12:9, we read of "the great dragon . . . that old serpent . . . which deceiveth the whole world".

God's Word is able to defeat Satan, as we saw with Jesus—and according to Martin Luther, "one little Word shall fell him".[122] Our job is to resist the devil, who we are told will then flee from us (James 4:7). We are partakers in this conflict.

Finally, if we are to "tread down" in this way, then our "feet" must be clean to start with. Like those who wore sandals in Jesus' day, our "feet" get sullied by the normal activities of life; hence the need for Christian fellowship where—whether physically, as a symbolic act, or not—we "wash each other's feet" by exhorting and praying for each other, a necessary part of the Christian life. As the disciples allowed Jesus to wash their feet (John 13:5-15), so we can wash others' feet and let them wash ours (I Tim. 5:10). This may be in practical matters to help others walk safely and securely. We are

---

121   Strong, s.v. "suntribō," 69.
122   Martin Luther, *Eine Feste Burg*, 1527.

to make "safe paths" for our feet (Heb. 12:13), which are to be "shod with the preparation of the gospel of peace" (Eph. 6:15). Symbolic of spiritual purity and preparedness, this footwear ensures that the enemy can see no sin in us; so God can bless, and the lame can be healed (Heb. 12:13).

Clean hands, clean feet, a pure heart (Matt. 5:8; John 13:10)—all prerequisites for us to "dwell in the secret place of the most High". Only then can we—undefeated—trample our spiritual foes "under feet".

CHAPTER 10

GOD THE DELIVERER

STROPHE FOUR

"Because he hath set his love upon me, therefore will I deliver him:
I will set him on high, because he hath known my name." (v. 14)

NOW THE PSALM TURNS a corner. Gone are the dangers, disasters, destructions, and predators. The language is now that of Divine love, a soliloquy from the Creator about His treasured, as if someone has asked Him, "So what are you going to do for this one who has stated his belief in You?" God stands back, thinks, smiles, and states, "Because he has done this, I am going to do all these for him."

He proclaims with increasing intensity eight plain statements of His compassionate intentions for His beloved. There is no judgement or chastisement here, only affirmation and hints of lavish plans beyond the believer's comprehension. The statements tumble out one after another, until with the final sweeping, powerful voice of a kindly King—one with total power to bless, order, and do all His heart's purpose—He states, "With long life will I satisfy him, and shew him my salvation." The matter is settled, the process begun. It remains only for the amazing, eternal significance of these pronouncements to sink in and become reality.

In this poem of dedication to the one who loves Him, God's first thought is of deliverance; and then seven more responses are added to the recipients who are loving God, knowing His name, and calling on Him. These are to set him on high, to answer him, to be with him in trouble, to deliver him, to honour him, to satisfy him with long life, and—in the grand finale—to show him His salvation. The string of promises in this strophe is based on only the three conditions: setting our love upon God, knowing His name, and calling upon Him.

If reciting these verses, we speak God's words after Him, think His thoughts, and proclaim them. Thus, we are drawn nearer to understanding Him and are better able to follow the command found in Ephesians 5:1 to "be ye therefore followers of God, as dear children". We will also then be focused on delivering those who love *us*, setting them up instead of pulling them down, answering their requests when they need help, being with them in trouble, delivering them, equipping them to do better, honouring them, helping them have a satisfied and fulfilled life, and showing them the way of salvation.

"Therefore" is inserted into the text to strengthen it. Nowadays, it would be doubling up on "because" (i.e., using "because" renders "therefore" redundant). Once again, in a chiastic construction such as verse fourteen—*Because he has done that, I will do this: I will do this, because he has done that*—the first statement is grammatically reversed in the second.

The key word here from our part of the deal is "love". God showed in verse one how to enter into and dwell in the secret place. The issue now is to stay there for the long term.

Three conditions are given to receive the promises from God:

1. Set our love on Him
2. Know His name
3. Call upon Him.

Eight phrases describe what He does:

1. Delivers
2. Sets on high
3. Answers
4. Is with us in trouble
5. Delivers (a different Hebrew word again)
6. Honours
7. Gives "long life"
8. Shows His salvation

We do three. God does eight. Whether we receive from Him depends on whether we set our love on Him. Again, the concept is circular: "We love Him, because He first loved us" (I John 4:19). His grace is free; and we respond by loving Him back—not earning His blessings by loving Him but with a mindset, a choice, to lift our heart to Him. *His* response is love. All this echoes the great commandment to "love the Lord thy God with all thy heart, and with all thy soul, and with all thy mind, and with all thy strength" (Mark 12:30).

But in verse fourteen of our psalm, a different word occurs than in the Deuteronomy 6:5 commandment, where the most common Hebrew word for "love" (to have affection for[123]), was used. Here in verse fourteen, it is another meaning—to cling, join, love, delight[124]—used eleven times in the concordance with its first usage referring to the love of a man for a woman (Gen. 34:8, "longeth") and several instances also denoting God's love for His people. For example, in the following verses, the translation is "delight":

- "The LORD did not set his love upon you, nor choose you, because you were more in number than any people." (Deut. 7:7)

---

123 Strong, s.v. "'âhab," 9.
124 Strong, s.v. "châshaq," 44.

- "The LORD had a delight[125] in thy fathers to love[126] them." (Deut. 10:15).
- "Thou hast in love to my soul delivered it from the pit of corruption: for thou hast cast all my sins behind thy back." (Isa. 38:17).

Psalm 91 refers to the lover of God, "because he hath set his love upon me". Job described this clinging, longing, joining, delighting, and desiring, stating, "He knoweth the way that I take: when he hath tried me, I shall come forth as gold. My foot hath held his steps, his way have I kept, and not declined. Neither have I gone back from the commandment of his lips; I have esteemed the words of his mouth more than my necessary food" (Job 23:10-12).

I mentioned earlier that at least twenty-one different Hebrew words are found for "deliver", which in its three instances in this psalm are translated differently each time. In Psalm 91:14, the word indicates slipping out, escaping, or being carried away safely.[127] Other occurrences in the Psalms include:

- "And the LORD shall help them, and deliver them: he shall deliver them from the wicked, and save them, because they trust in him" (37:40)
- "O deliver me from the deceitful and unjust man" (43:1)
- "Deliver me, O my God, out of the hand of the wicked, out of the hand of the unrighteous and cruel man" (71:4)
- "Deliver the poor and needy: rid them out of the hand of the wicked" (82:4).

God can deliver His people from the depredations of the deceitful, the unjust, the unrighteous, the cruel, and the wicked.

In the Lord's Prayer, we pray "hallowed be thy name" (Matt. 6:9). But His name cannot be hallowed (i.e., honoured by holding sacred) without the

---

125 Ibid.
126 Strong, s.v. "'âhab," 9.
127 Strong, s.v. "pâlat," 95.

"hallower" first *knowing* it. To love Him and to know His name (His position, honour, authority, and character) are the only requirements given. The psalmist did not fulfil these requirements to *get* God's favour. Instead, God *gave* him favour by his voluntarily fulfilling them.

The first mention of proclaiming the name of the LORD is where God said to Moses that He would "proclaim the name of the LORD before thee" (Exod. 33:19). On the mount when He and Moses were alone, God "descended in the cloud . . . and proclaimed the name of the LORD" (Exod. 34:5)—proclaiming that He *was* some things and that He *would do*, and *would not do*, some things. He *was* "merciful and gracious, longsuffering, and abundant in goodness and truth". He *would* be "keeping mercy . . . forgiving iniquity and transgression and sin". He *would not* acquit those who would not come to Him for forgiveness, but in fact would be "visiting the iniquity of the fathers upon the children . . . unto the third and to the fourth generation" (Exod. 34:6-7).

This helps us understand what knowing His name entails. It involves understanding His character. His names illustrate His character; and all Scripture describes His acts, which accord with that character.

The Old Testament speaks of the coming of the Messiah, and a string of titles is given Him throughout Scripture. But His name in Hebrew is a name, not a title; and in the New Testament, the full Greek name is *kuriôs*[128] *Iēsŏus*[129] *Christôs*[130]—the Lord Jesus Christ. Here is the answer to the question, how to "know" God's name. To honour Him and know the One *behind* the name is, in one sense, the same as knowing anyone. If you know them, then you speak convincingly of them in a way that assures others you have spent enough time with them to understand how they think, what their motivations are, and what their personality and character are like. How we do that with God is threefold: reading His Word, speaking to Him, and listening as He speaks to us—like picking up on the feelings of our friends, those we know, and

---

128 Strong, s.v. "kuriôs," 44.
129 Strong, s.v. "Iēsŏus," 37.
130 Strong, s.v. "Christôs," 78.

sensing their hearts through spending time with them and talking to them. The key to knowing God is to meet Him now. In seeking Him, we sense Him also calling us, and we respond.

Psalm 9:10 emphasizes the connection between knowing Him and trusting Him: "And they that know thy name will put their trust in thee." Isaiah 26:8 also speaks of this relationship: "The desire of our soul is to thy name, and to the remembrance of thee."

Knowing His name means setting our love upon Him. Being set on high means being delivered and instated or reinstated into a safe place, as seen in the following verses:

- "But I am poor and sorrowful: let thy salvation, O God, set me up on high" (Psalm 69:29).
- "Yet setteth he the poor on high from affliction" (Psalm 107:41).

On "high" is where the otherwise vulnerable can be secure from attack or oppression. The phrase is used many times in Scripture, referring also to God (Psalm 113:5) and Jesus, "the Son of God most high" (Luke 8:28), Who also told His disciples that they would be "endued with power from on high" (Luke 24:49).

It refers not only to a physical place of security or prosperity—it can be that—but also, and more importantly for the believer, a secure *spiritual* place, inaccessible to all spiritual opposition. How we come into this now is through calling on the name of the Lord (John 1:12), Whom God sent not only for salvation (Matt. 1:21) but also as the surety that God is with us (Emmanuel, "God with us"—Isa. 7:14; Matt. 1:23).

We are to trust in this name (Matt. 12:21) and call on it, for "whosoever shall call on the name of the Lord shall be saved" (Acts 2:21). We find "remission of sins" (Acts 10:43), justification (I Cor. 6:11), and eternal life (I John 5:13). The result is the willingness to wholeheartedly serve God. "For then will I turn to the people a pure language, that they may all call upon the name of the LORD, to serve him with one consent" (Zeph. 3:9).

His name is above all others (Phil. 2:9-10; Heb. 1:4); and when we are His and follow Him, we are raised up together and made "to sit together in heavenly places in Christ Jesus" (Eph. 2:6).

"Name" in verse fourteen is the common word for name, implying also honor, authority, and character.[131] We have seen the four names of God given in the first two verses, with two being repeated in verse nine.

'Elyôwn is the name of God especially used in His connection with the peoples of the whole world. For example, in Genesis 19, this name was used when Abraham met Melchizedek—the priest of the most High God and also, it would seem, a non-Israelite. The book of Daniel, set in Medo-Persia, also uses this name numerous times. The other name from verse one was discussed earlier.

Yehôvâh[132] ("I AM THAT I AM" in Exodus 3:14) is used twice in Psalm 91 (v. 2 and 9) connected to the phrase "my refuge" and associated with the covenant-giving God. It is seen in "LORD God" (as in Gen. 2), the name of God the Creator speaking to and dealing with us.[133] As verse two of Psalm 91 says, "I will say of the LORD, He is my refuge and my fortress: my God; in him will I trust."

By coming into relationship with Him we may use this name. It is essentially Who we are connecting to when we use the title "Lord". Jesus identified with it, as seen in His words in John 8:58—"Before Abraham was, I am"—and in John 18:6—"I am he." And He implies it in His statements of "But I say unto you" in Matthew 5:22, 28, 32, 34, 39, and 44, where He showed His authority to clarify and extend the meanings of the Torah. Jesus the Lord is our Refuge, we "who have fled for refuge to lay hold upon the hope set before us" (Heb. 6:18).

---

131   Strong, s.v. "shêm," 117.
132   Strong, s.v. "Yehôvâh," 47.
133   Rev. W. Pascoe Goard, *The Names of God* (Durham: The Covenant Publishing Co. Ltd., 2010).

The old patriarchs were familiar with God as the Almighty (*Shadday*[134]), God (*ĕlôhîym*[135]), the "LORD" (*Yehôvâh*[136]) (i.e. His "relational" name when addressed, prayed to, or spoken about), the Most High (*Elyôwn*[137]), and the Lord (*'Ădônây*[138]). But the full character expressed in His name was not known until Moses' burning bush experience. God's commitment to His people as their faithful, covenant-keeping Redeemer was freshly revealed to Moses (Exod. 2:24-25; 3:1-22; 6:2-3); and at Mount Sinai, His laws were given in clear written form. They were the catalyst for us to connect to Him, not by obeying them in our own strength but by understanding through their authority over us that we are incapable of keeping them to God's satisfaction and therefore must come to Him in faith and repentance to fulfil them.

The names are also joined together sometimes, as in "God most high" (Psalm 57:2), "the most high God" (Psalm 78:56), and "LORD most high" (Psalm 7:17).

So in strophes one and two of Psalm 91, we have, chronologically:

- "The most High" of all nations (also in verse nine of strophe three)
- "The Almighty", blesser, protector and provider
- "The LORD", with whom we have fellowship (also in verse nine of strophe three)
- "My God", the originator of all things.

"The LORD" refers to the One Who, following our repentance and trust, becomes our Saviour. John the Baptist's message in Mark 1:3 and Luke 3:4 of "the voice of one crying in the wilderness, Prepare ye the way of the Lord, make his paths straight" and in John 1:23 of "the voice of one crying in the wilderness. Make straight the way of the Lord, as said the prophet Esaias" come from Isaiah 40:3: "Prepare ye the way of the LORD, make straight in

---

134 Strong, s.v. "Shadday," 113.
135 Strong, s.v. "ĕlôhîym," 12.
136 Strong, s.v. "Yehôvâh," 47.
137 Strong, s.v. "'elyôwn," 88.
138 Strong, s.v. "'Ădônây," 8.

the desert a highway for our God". John used *kuriôs* and Isaiah *Yehôvâh*, but the quote shows that they are identical in meaning—"LORD" points to Jesus. In its verse nine reiteration, this name is followed again by the words "my refuge", affirming the connection between relationship and refuge.

Then comes again the last name mentioned, which is also the *first* name in the psalm—*Elyôwn*, the One reaching out to all the peoples of the earth and commanding them to repent and believe.

So verse fourteen is speaking of God's character and *all* His names, but especially His relational name; and it is the same God revealed in the New Testament as our refuge. There we have the title of respect for a father, a master, a ruler, or even a stranger—*kuriôs*, which from the book of Acts on is used primarily in reference to Jesus. When rebuking Satan for trying to tempt Him, Jesus spoke of "the Lord thy God" (Matt. 4:7, 10); and I Peter 1:25 equates the term "Lord" with God in "But the word of the Lord endureth forever."

In summary, to know Him is to know His name and His character as revealed in *all* His names and titles. The presence of His Holy Spirit within us helps us understand His nature. Psalm 145:1-2 speak of praising God *and* His name as synonymous ideas: "I will extol thee, my God, O king; and I will bless thy name for ever and ever. Every day will I bless thee; and I will praise thy name for ever and ever."

Next, we read in verse fifteen, "He shall call upon me, and I will answer him: I will be with him in trouble; I will deliver him, and honour him". Answered prayer, God's presence, deliverance, honour—all result from calling upon Him. The words for deliver so far have been to snatch away[139], to carry away safely[140], and now, finally to deliver by pulling off[141] (but also can be about strengthening or equipping for a fight). Other places it is found include:

---

139   Strong, s.v. "nâtsal," 80.
140   Strong, s.v. "pâlat," 95.
141   Strong, s.v. "châlats," 40.

- "Return, O LORD, deliver my soul" (Psalm 6:4)
- "And call upon me in the day of trouble: I will deliver thee, and thou shalt glorify me" (Psalm 50:15)
- "Consider mine affliction, and deliver me: for I do not forget thy law" (Psalm 119:153)
- "Deliver me, O LORD from the evil man" (Psalm 140:1).

David did call upon God. "Give ear to my prayer O God: and hide not thyself from my supplication. Attend unto me, and hear me: I mourn in my complaint, and make a noise; Because of the voice of the enemy, because of the oppression of the wicked" (Psalm 55:1-3).

Psalm 121 also has similarities to Psalm 91, starting with, "I will lift up mine eyes unto the hills . . . My help cometh from the LORD" (vv. 1-2). First, we lift up our eyes, figuratively speaking, to God; that is, we turn to Him, look to Him, focus on Him, gaze upon Him, and give all our attention to Him, for that is where we find the secret place. We acknowledge to God, ourselves, and others where our true help comes from, affirming our trust in Him. The first part of verse three of Psalm 121—"He will not suffer thy foot to be moved"—compares with verse twelve of Psalm 91. The results of being kept and preserved come from our first decision, namely to lift up our eyes "to the hills", metaphorical of our first move towards the real Source of help.

"Call"[142] gives the idea of "accosting a person met". Essentially, it refers to prayer. "Call upon me in the day of trouble: I will deliver thee and thou shalt glorify me" (Psalm 50:15).

- As for me, I will call upon God; and the LORD shall save me. Evening and morning, and at noon, will I pray, and cry aloud: and he shall hear my voice. He hath delivered my soul in peace from the battle that was against me: for there were many with me. (Psalm 55:16-18)

---

142 Strong, s.v. "qârâ'," 104.

- The LORD is nigh unto all them that call upon him, to all them that call upon him in truth. He will fulfil the desire of them that fear him: he also will hear their cry, and will save them. The LORD preserveth all them that love him: but all the wicked will he destroy. (Psalm 145:18-20)

- For I know the thoughts that I think toward you, saith the LORD, thoughts of peace, and not of evil, to give you an expected end. Then shall ye call upon me, and ye shall go and pray unto me, and I will hearken unto you. And ye shall seek me, and find me, when ye shall search for me with all your heart. (Jer. 29:11-13)

In all these examples, God is near us. He hears, saves, releases, and preserves us. He is with us in trouble, adversity, affliction, anguish, distress, and tribulation. We have a double blessing—deliverance and honour.

"Answer"[143] means to heed, pay attention to, and respond. "I will answer him" is God's reassuring promise. So when we call out to Him, He will respond by being with us in trouble and delivering and honouring us.

---

143 Strong, s.v. "ânâh," 90.

LONG LIFE, SALVATION

STROPHE FOUR (CONT.)

"With long life will I satisfy him, and shew him my salvation." (v. 16)

AT FIRST GLANCE, THE first clause of this verse seems to give assurance of a long life, and so the longevity interpretation is the first we would naturally consider. The original language suggests more, though. Should it be threescore and ten years or fourscore "by reason of strength" as mentioned in Psalm 90:10? Or should it be open-ended, relative to time and place? We can note that the latter verse, in the context of Israel's wilderness wanderings, adds, "Yet is their strength labour and sorrow". But we do not find the same mood in Psalm 91.

Of course, "long" is different according to context. On the shorter side, in various places, at various times in history, sixty, fifty, even forty years or less have been expected age lengths. On the longer side, places such as Okinawa and Sardinia regularly have people living into their nineties and early hundreds. Ninety remains a grand old age in most of the world; but long ago, people lived into the hundreds. Methuselah is recorded to have lived the longest, making it to 969 years (Gen. 5:27); and others then also lived to extraordinary ages. We find such numbers astonishing now because we are unused to them. Our physical bodies—our genetics—have declined, and we are accustomed to today's normal lifespans. And while science struggles to fully explain the ultimate cause of natural death, Scripture clearly attributes it to the Fall.

Moses lived to 120 years, and Aaron, his older brother, to 123. Moses' "eye was not dim, nor his natural force abated" (Deut. 34:7), referring to his vigour. This raises the question of how he died. He knew he was old, as we sense from his acknowledgement in Deuteronomy 31:2 that his confidence to lead the people had diminished; and he could no longer "go out and come in"— referring to his ability to lead (Num. 27:17; I Kings 3:7). Since the Bible does not reveal how he died, it can only be guessed. Perhaps at an appointed time, his heart simply stopped beating. Interestingly, while fourscore years is still considered a fairly old age, records of the oldest people nowadays often show them being a few years short of 120, the longest proven being a little over 122 (Jean Louise Calment, 1875-1997).

Was Moses an exception, or was his age the new maximum? Sarah, Abraham, Joshua, and David in the Old Testament and Zacharias and Elisabeth in the New Testament are all depicted as being "old and stricken in years" (Josh. 13:1). Anna the prophetess, whose age is given as eighty-four, was "of a great age" (Luke 2:36). "Stricken" implies being struck by something, but this is not necessarily so in the original languages in relation to longevity. Rather, it means advanced in years, implying nothing in particular about health.

Joshua, at eighty-five, was as strong as the day that Moses sent him out forty-five years earlier. "As my strength was then, even so is my strength now, for war, both to go out, and to come in" (Josh. 14:10-11). His confidence was in God (Psalm 34:2; 44:8). Those closely following God seemed to experience a similar type of strength. When he died, Joshua was 110. In King David's later rule, however, we read of Barzillai, "a very aged man, even fourscore years old" (II Sam. 19:32). Perhaps life's stresses in that time of conflict had taken their toll. Contrariwise, years later, the righteous priest Jehoiada lived to 130. So in those times, too, the term "old" seems to have also needed context.

Elisha died of sickness at an unknown age yet was a man with a double portion of Elijah's anointing (II Kings 2:9; 13:14), and Paul left Trophimus at Miletum sick (II Tim. 4:20). And we do not know whether he recovered or how long he lived. Many in the early church died young from persecution. Again, context alone can assist us to navigate our way through apparent scriptural contradictions. Consider the words of Jesus in Mark 10:52, and how, while some were martyred, other heroes "through faith . . . obtained promises"—perhaps parallel promises to those of Psalm 91, as mentioned in Hebrews (Heb. 11:33ff).

The phrase "long life" in verse sixteen consists of "long"[144] and "life"[145]. In the book of Proverbs, weight is given, in a similar manner, to both quality and longevity, as in Proverbs 3:2: "For length of days and long life[146] and peace, shall they add to thee." This is the result of remembering God's law and keeping His commandments from the heart. "Long life" in Psalm 91:16 is the same as "length of days" in Proverbs 3:2. Psalm 21:4 states, "He asked life of thee, and thou gavest it him, even length of days for ever and ever". And Proverbs 3:16 says, "Length of days is in her right hand".

This is also, in reference to wisdom, in Proverbs 4:5-13, especially verse ten: "Hear, O my son, and receive my sayings; and the years of thy life shall be many." Deuteronomy uses the phrase in speaking of God Himself being the length of our days (30:20) and our days being either prolonged (Deut. 4:40; 5:16, 33; 6:2; 11:9; 22:7; 32:47) or not, if there is disobedience (4:26; 30:18). The Hebrew word for "long" comes from the word for "prolong". Hence the phrase in question in Psalm 91 could read "length of days". The query remains as to why the translators (as in other translations too) used "long life". "Length of days", indeed, does not, in the first instance, suggest longevity nor flow quite as well as "long life"; in a literal sense, it means little to us today since we all have twenty-four hours wherever we are. Days, then, must be able to be "long" in a figurative sense.

---

144 Strong, s.v. "'ôrek," 16.
145 Strong, s.v. "yôwm," 48.
146 Strong, s.v. "chay," 38.

Other expressions analogous to "long life" or "length of days", though using different Hebrew words, speak likewise. Ten times the book of Deuteronomy has "prolong" plus "days" (e.g., "prolong your days", "prolong his days", "thy days may be prolonged"), all from obeying God's commandments. It is used in a different context with reference to the Messiah in Isaiah 53:10, but terms about lengthening of days often appear as metaphors for long life. The word from which the name "Joseph" is derived *also* means to add, augment, or prolong[147] and is used in Psalm 61:6: "Thou wilt prolong the king's life: and his years as many generations", where the synonymous parallelism infers duration, literally adding days to days. Proverbs 10:27, using the matching word, links the idea of adding days to life in the first clause with numbers of years in the second in a characteristically contrasting, antithetical parallelism: "The fear of the LORD prolongeth days: but the years of the wicked shall be shortened."

The nuance here is that the fear of the Lord tends to give more life both in length *and* quality than would otherwise be the case, while wickedness tends to shorten life expectancy. In contrast, Ecclesiastes 7:15 compares the wicked man "that prolongeth his life in his wickedness" with the just man "that perisheth in his righteousness". The same word in Ecclesiastes 8:12 speaks of a hypothetical sinner whose "days" are prolonged, probably referring to his being unaware that his sins will ever catch up with him, since verse thirteen reminds us that "it shall not be well with the wicked, neither shall he prolong his days, which are as a shadow; because he feareth not before God". The statement in Ecclesiastes 9:2, "all things come alike to all", shows that this book reveals its wisdom best when carefully exegeted.

The ungodly *may* grow to an advanced age, but their prospects at the end of life are significantly less desirable; for though they prosper and increase in riches, yet they will be "brought into desolation, as in a moment! . . . utterly consumed with terrors" (Psalm 73:19), as we saw in Psalm 2.

---

147   Strong, s.v. "yâçaph," 50.

A further answer as to why the translators of the King James Version used "long life" and not "length of days" is in the verb phrase, always the controlling part of any sentence. The future tense "will . . . satisfy" reveals that a focus of the clause is satisfaction pertaining to quality of life. The word means to fill to satisfaction (i.e., satiate, have plenty of or enough); and while debateable which is more important—quality or length—the word indicates full sufficiency. God may well be speaking about joy and satisfaction through sufficiency. Physical needs, desires, or material comforts come and go according to factors beyond our control; so they may not be the focus here, since we read elsewhere that God will take care of those.

In fact, this word "satisfied" has many applications in Scripture, positive and negative. Both translations, "satisfaction" and "full", come in many contexts. People can be satisfied with or full of (sometimes in metaphorical and occasionally in negative ways) food, honey, bread, the finest of the wheat, marrow, good, goodness, years, days, riches, honour, wealth, children, fruit of the mouth, increase of the lips, their own devices, their own ways, trouble, "tossings to and fro",[148] contempt, scorning, bitterness, reproach, shame, or confusion. Hell and destruction are never "full", and God can be fed up ("full") with the sacrifices of burnt offerings by insincere religionists. But there can also be "fulness" of joy in God's presence, "in thy presence is fulness of joy" (Psalm 16:11).

I mentioned earlier that Jehoiada, who lived 130 years, died "full of days", being buried in the city of David "among the kings, because he had done good in Israel, both toward God, and toward his house" (II Chron. 24:15-16). If we, too, live in the fulfilment of Psalm 91 in that secret place, whatever length of life we end up with will nevertheless give us sufficient reason to glorify God; and our life will satisfy us regardless of its length.

There are other words for "life" in the Old Testament, such as *chay*,[149] as above, which Proverbs 3:2 and Genesis 2:7 use: "God . . . breathed into his

---

148 Job 7:4.
149 Strong, s.v. "chay," 38.

nostrils the breath of life" (Gen. 2:7). And *nephesh*[150] is used in Ruth 4:15: "And he shall be unto thee a restorer of thy life." Psalm 91:16 gives us *yôwm*,[151] from the idea of the warmth of the day and "to be hot", clearly connected with the sun's energy and in both Hebrew and Chaldean meaning "a day" ("and God called the light Day"—Gen. 1:5). Throughout the Old Testament, with only several exceptions, this word is used for "day".

However, in the phrase "long life", it is used in another context in addition to this final verse, in God's commendation of King Solomon's prayer for understanding and discernment, rather than for selfish matters such as riches and long life. The story is related in two passages in both of which "long" is *rab*:[152]

- "Because thou . . . hast not asked for thyself long life . . . but hast asked for thyself understanding to discern judgement" (1 Kings 3:11)
- "Because . . . thou . . . neither yet hast asked long life." (II Chron. 1:11)

Solomon asked for "an understanding heart to judge thy people, that I may discern between good and bad" (I Kings 3:9), or, in the version in II Chronicles 1:10, "give me now wisdom and knowledge". Because he did not ask for a "long life" (i.e., length of days or a satisfied life) *or* for riches, honour, and wealth, but rather asked for wisdom, knowledge, and understanding, God gave him his request and then *added in* the riches and the honour. However, we do not know how long King Solomon lived. It is conjectured to have been between sixty to eighty years.

We should follow Solomon's example, not asking for our own self-centred desires but giving priority to wisdom and knowledge. When he strayed from God, however, he missed life's meaning and lost the satisfaction of life (see Eccles. 1:1-11).

---

150 Strong, s.v. "nephesh," 80.
151 Strong, s.v. "yôwm," 48.
152 Strong, s.v. "rab," 106.

Should we then aim for a long life or only as much as will satisfy us? While "satisfy" has many applications, it cannot easily be pinned down to one context, so does not exclude the spiritual satisfaction that salvation brings. Other legitimate contentment might apply. God knows our allotted span, and at the end of it should be a sense of fulfilment that we have done all He asked of us—provided we lived for Him. According to Jesus' teachings, this is not to be grasped at: "For whosoever will save his life shall lose it: and whosoever will lose his life for my sake shall find it" (Matt. 16:25). The irony, though, is that by letting go of our sinful nature and our "right" to control, we discover abundant life: "I am come that they might have life, and that they might have it more abundantly" (John 10:10).

Psalm 91's meaning of "long life" is positive: "Abraham . . . died in a good old age, an old man, and full of years" (Gen. 25:8); Isaac, was "old and full of days" (Gen. 35:29); David was "old and full of days" (I Chron. 23:1), dying "in a good old age, full of days, riches, and honour" (I Chron. 29:28). In all these, "full" [153] has the sense of being satisfied.

The question, then, is whether it should be long or satisfied, or both. The term *'ôrek yôwm* appears to mean both but with a focus on spiritual satisfaction or "fulness of joy" coming from God's presence, as in Psalm 92:12-14, which speaks of the righteous flourishing "like the palm tree . . . in the courts of our God" and bringing forth fruit in old age (see Psalm 1). To "flourish" means to bloom, like a bud turning into a flower.

"Long life", then, is justified as a translation for Psalm 91:16, as are "length of days" and "long life" elsewhere, such as in the I Kings and II Chronicles passages. What it says in English (i.e., that a long life in the sense of a ripe old age is possible) is consistent with the tenor of the Hebrew as well as current usage. This verse points us towards a long life, though perhaps without inferring categorically that *all* who believe will automatically live to an advanced age, given factors such as environment and choice. But whether

---

153   All use the Hebrew word *sâbêa'* ("satiated"), as considered above.

"short" or "long", satisfaction from God's blessings (and our right choices) is certain. Consider also the five-fold benefits given in Psalm 103:1-5 for those in covenant with Him: forgiveness, healing, redemption, protection (lit. "crowning" or encircling, e.g., Psalm 8:5), and renewal.

This final verse is a dramatic, definitive declaration of the Psalm's overall meaning, culminating in the statement about God showing the believer His salvation. It reflects a parallel triumphant finish to the other famous psalm used in so many contexts, Psalm 23: "Surely goodness and mercy shall follow me all the days of my life:[154] and I will dwell in the house of the LORD for ever" (v. 6). The second half of this speaks of the ultimate, eternal fulfilment of "long life".

"Shew" is the same as "see" in verse eight, but meaning "cause to see" here. Salvation can be physical deliverance, as when Moses said to the children of Israel, "Stand still, and see the salvation of the LORD" (Exod. 14:13). Or it can be an instatement into a better condition or the process of being rescued, as in Psalm 69:29: "But I am poor and sorrowful: let thy salvation, O God, set me up on high". Or it can be spiritual salvation (I Peter 1:9) coming through repentance, faith, and verbal confession (Luke 19:9; Rom. 1:16; 10:10). The word here in the last verse of Psalm 91 (i.e., "salvation",[155]) speaks of liberation and victory in battle (I Sam. 14:45). Associated words also translated "salvation" are found, for example, in Psalm 62:7[156], Psalm 40:16[157], and (for "save" and "saviour") in Psalm 106:21 and Isaiah 60:16[158].

With the Greek words of the New Testament for "save" and "salvation"[159] [160], we find the connotations all, again, being about safety, freedom, and wholeness. The New Testament points to the Deliverer, Who Himself rescues or brings

---

154   I.e., the satisfaction of the godly as in Psalm 91.
155   Strong, s.v. "yeshûw'âh," 53.
156   Strong, s.v. "yêsha'," 53.
157   Strong, s.v. "teshû'âh," 126.
158   Strong, s.v. "yâsha'," 53.
159   Strong, s.v. "sōtēria," 70.
160   Strong, s.v. "sōzō," 70.

physical, moral, or spiritual safety. The ancient Greek and Hebrew languages have a relational history, with Greek used in the Septuagint (LXX), the most important translation of the Hebrew Old Testament, and also as a lingua franca at the time of the early church. Hence, these Greek words would likely have been as well known to the early church as the Hebrew.

Psalm 91 ends appropriately: "With long life will I satisfy him, and shew him my salvation." Life's ultimate fulfilment is salvation—eternal life in the Lord Jesus Christ Who Himself is our Deliverer and our Saviour—our *yeshûw'âh*. Like Psalm 2, this final verse reveals Him to us.

CONCLUSION TO PSALM 91

REALISATION OF PSALM 91 is contingent upon us living in "the secret place of the most High" and "under the shadow of the Almighty". Within that context, its assurances apply; and provided this first condition is met, its blessings remain valid today and forever. We trust in God not for a list of benefits but because it rests on us as His created beings to make the effort, regardless of reward, to love Him with all our heart, soul, mind, and strength (Mark 12:30) and to begin that process by placing our full confidence in His dependability. We are to set our love upon Him as we are encouraged to do in verse fourteen and elsewhere in the Psalms (e.g., Psalm 31:23: "O love the LORD, all ye his saints").

Using Scripture as a talisman, a sort of good luck charm, violates God's laws. This is because the veneration of any object or objects, even including writings on paper or on a screen, outside of their original purpose, can become an idolatrous act. Our trust and worship are to be towards the Creator Himself alone.

Before or during a crisis, and perhaps as a last resort, people sometimes look for security in Scripture such as Psalm 91 in the hope of relief. But God and His Word cannot be treated as trinkets or enchantments to use at our convenience. When the devil misquoted Psalm 91:11, Jesus did not engage him in a dispute about the original meanings of the Scriptures or the fact that they were being misrepresented; but rather, He used the Word itself to strike down his adversary in one blow. "It is written . . . thou shalt not tempt the Lord thy God" (Matt.4:7). "Tempt" means to test, prove, or try out. Thus Jesus immediately identified Satan's motive to entice Him to "prove" God and to do so on Satan's own terms. But using *any* portion of Scripture to "try out" God in unbelief only invites His condemnation.

Furthermore, while the memorisation of any part of God's Word is to be encouraged, to commit it to memory or to quote it is only the beginning. More is needed—namely, connection with the Divine Writer, *after which*, with His Word hidden in our hearts, our life purpose can be discovered. Memorising assists that, of course; and meditating (in its biblical sense) on Scripture helps draw us closer to understanding the Word. "Thy words were found, and I did eat them; and thy word was unto me the joy and rejoicing of mine heart: for I am called by thy name, O LORD God of hosts" (Jer. 15:16).

So the Creator must *first* be known and accepted as Saviour and Lord, and then His Word living within our hearts will feed the resultant new life. With the promises and assurances of this psalm to back us up, all that we need do is make sure we are in that secret place and then work out our faith from there.

We may ask, what if I get sick, or catch a virus, or have an accident, or if those who hate me get the better of me? In each case, practical solutions summon us. We can look after our health, get exercise, find appropriate medical advice, supplement our diet, eat healthy food, drive carefully, and show generosity and love to our enemies. Having done everything possible, as God expects of us, including exercising our faith, we can do no more, and so worrying is no longer necessary. What is beyond our control is *never* beyond His. And our faith can increase. By getting into the place of spiritual rest, of abiding in Christ Jesus, of loving Him, all our human fears and anxieties which sometimes arise in our lives can be brought to God and left with Him.

The apostle Paul knew the secret place of God's presence. While confessing once in the middle of his Macedonian ministry that he and his co-workers were "troubled on every side; without were fightings, within were fears" (II Cor. 7:5), he also said, "I am filled with comfort, I am exceeding joyful in all our tribulation" (II Cor. 7:4). But will this passage of biblical poetic-prose, Psalm 91, guarantee protection and immunity from problems to all who believe it?

The assurance is certainly one of protection in the context of the usual *and* the unexpected challenges and problems of life. But this study has shown that it is much more. It is about a connection with the Creator. We become tempted to disbelieve, to question. Aches and pains, weaknesses, wear and tear, and opposing messages everywhere try to convince us that it is unreal or impractical. Yesterday, we were strong; today, we are weak; today, we are weak; tomorrow, we are strong again. This is life. Yet God remains the same—always strong, always consistent. And His Word remains reliable.

Our fallen nature naturally contends with our spirit and tries to persuade us to abandon the quest for—and the summons from God to—faith and the riches of His wisdom. It pulls us towards worldly concerns. Verses such as, "If ye had faith as a grain of mustard seed" (Luke 17:6) indeed challenge us. And we are further tested by dark, seductive voices whispering, "Impossible! False! Nonsense!" In these moments, more than anything, we need understanding. And we need to take up the challenge that, while Paul's words "O wretched man that I am!" (Rom. 7:24) may likewise ring true for us, yet we can triumphantly echo that unknown father's words: "Lord, I believe; help thou mine unbelief" (Mark 9:24). And then listen for God's message to us.

While we logically expect the normal to happen in the natural, we can also expect the supernatural to happen in the normal. Our spirit and soul can respond to the stimulus of God's Word and Spirit as we say no to the pull of unbelief. We have seen how Psalm 91 deals with major issues—plagues, pestilences, traps, terrors, arrows, destructions, dying thousands, lions, serpents, the dragon—and while challenging all these, we are at the same time pointed to a safe place, a protective covering, a fortress, a refuge, a shield, deliverance, angels, answers to prayer, honour, long life, and salvation. We are reminded that nothing is too big for God, Who can be entrusted with all our concerns, small and large.

I encourage you to regularly read and further explore Psalm 91. Choose to believe it, putting your full confidence in the One Who inspired it and Who still speaks to us through it.

CHAPTER 12

A SUMMARY / PARAPHRASE OF PSALM 91

OF TREMENDOUS VALUE WHEN memorising Scripture is to summarise with your own words (naturally, however, without losing the meaning). As a young Christian, I appreciated the Navigators' Scripture memory training booklets, which encouraged rewording and rephrasing as an aid to memory. Based on the word studies made here and with all that has been considered above, a précis of Psalm 91's free-verse poetry and prose is offered below. ("Will" and "shall" are used interchangeably.)

STROPHE 1

He who sits down and settles under the shelter of the Most High Supreme God shall remain under the shadow of the Almighty.

STROPHE 2

I will say of the Great covenant-keeping I AM, "He is my shelter and my defence, my Creator, in whom I will trust".

STROPHE 3

Surely he shall snatch you away from the snare of the fowler, and from the devastating plague. He will cover you over with his feathers, and under his wings you will trust: his truth shall be your shield and buckler. You will not fear any sudden, startling alarm at night, nor any flying arrow by day, nor any plague that walks in darkness, nor any destruction that swells up at midday. A thousand shall fall at your side and ten thousand at your right hand, but it will not come near you. Only with your eyes will you look, deeply consider, and perceive the reckoning which shall fall upon the troublemakers who violate God's laws.

Because you have made the LORD who is my place of shelter and hope, even the most High, your Retreat, no adversity or calamity will happen to you or even approach you, neither will any affliction come near your home. For he will appoint his angels to have guardianship over you, to hedge you about, protect, and attend to you in all your ways. They will lift you up in their hands, in case you dash your foot on a stone. You will tread upon the lion and adder: the young lion and the dragon you will trample under your feet.

STROPHE 4

Because he has longed for, delighted in, and clung to me, I will cause him to escape: I will set him on high in a safe, strong place because he has acknowledged my name, authority, and character. He will call out to me, and I will respond to him: I will be with him in trouble; I will deliver him by equipping him with what he needs to fight a good fight, and I will honour him. With long life will I satisfy him, and show him my salvation.

CHAPTER 13

PRAYER

PRAYING THROUGH PSALM 91 might go something like this:

Lord, I thank You that I live in Your secret place and stay safely under Your shadow. Thank You that You are my Refuge, my Fortress, and my God. I trust in You. Thank You that You deliver me out of life's unseen snares and plagues. Thank You that You cover me with Your feathers and that by living under Your wings, I have refuge.

Thank You that Your truth is a double shield and that I need fear no nighttime terrors, daytime arrows, unseen pestilences, or destructions. And even though thousands of people fall on both sides of me, none of those things can come near me. I know that the reward of the wicked will be clearly seen in due time as a warning and revelation of Your righteous judgements. Thank You that because I have made You my Refuge and Habitation, no evil will befall me or plague come near my home. Thank You that You give your angels charge over me to keep me in all my ways and that they bear me up in their hands, even if I make an inadvertent mistake.

Thank You that I may tread upon "lions" and "adders", and trample over "young lions" and even the "dragon", and those spiritual forces of evil which hate and oppose me. Thank You, too, that when I set my love upon You, You deliver me; and when I know

Your name, You set me on high. Thank You that when I call upon You, You answer me; You are with me in trouble; and You deliver, honour, and satisfy me, adding quality to each day and a "long life", however long You choose that to be. Thank You that You show me spiritual safety, protection, preservation, deliverance, and wholeness—and thank You that You show me Jesus. Amen.

CHAPTER 14

PERSONALISED DECLARATION

SAYING OUT LOUD PSALMS such as these, or singing them if you have a tune, is a powerful means of helping make sure that the truths do not remain theory alone but become practical, too. By personalising a Scripture in this way, nothing is added or taken away from it; but rather, our intention is harmonised with those truths by clear verbal assertion. Highlighting the meaning enhances our faith. The psalmist himself appears to have done this in verses two and nine of Psalm 91 when saying "my refuge", thus personalising previous revelations such as "The eternal God is *thy* refuge" (Deut. 33:27). We can now also say, "He will deliver *me* from the snare of the fowler, and from the noisome pestilence . . . *I* shall tread upon the lion and adder", etc. Or a wider-ranging declaration, using "we", could go as follows: *"We that dwell in the secret place of the most High shall abide under the shadow of the Almighty. We will say of the LORD, He is our refuge and our fortress: our God; in him will we trust"* (etc.).

In Psalm 2:7, Jesus said, "The Lord hath said unto me". What has the Lord said to you in these psalms? Have they helped to make your fears unnecessary and given fresh perspective on the world you live in? Having finished these two studies, you may like to consider doing a comparable study with other sections of Scripture, perhaps a page of rough notes, a look into the original languages, a research project about how the early church fathers approached a passage, or a consideration of their practical application or literary value.

POSTSCRIPT

KAREL VAN DER TOORN, in *Scribal Culture and the Making of the Hebrew Bible*, speaks of three colophons: the ones in Psalm 1, Proverbs 1, and Hosea 14:9 (preface, preface, and postscript respectively) and the fact that all of them are invitations to reading: "Righteousness comes from reading, and the very act of reading [the Scriptures] amounts almost to proof of righteousness".[161]

The delineations in those colophons of the "righteous", "wise", "prudent", and "godly" contrasted with the "transgressors", "scorners", "fools", and "ungodly" are derived from observation of how those individuals have responded to the Divine will as revealed in His written Word. They and other similar passages are encouragements for God's people to read, hear, and "mutter" (Psalm 1:2, transl. "meditate") the Word. For in its pages are found the wisdom, prudence, understanding, knowledge, and intelligence that has transformed people and cultures, creating contexts for constructive advancements in every area of life.

Imputed righteousness remains the crucial starting place for our journey of faith, but practical righteousness (originally "right-wiseness")—that is, right living—appears to primarily emerge from environments where not only faith is valued but also reading and study. Reflecting on these wonderful psalms, along with the rest of the Bible, and reading them in a version, whatever that may be, that satisfies your desire for quality literature will enhance every aspect of your life.

---

161   Van der Toorn, 258.

Psalm 2 gives perspective in the face of massive worldwide turmoil, showing why events are taking place as they are and how God can work within those events and ultimately resolve them. Psalm 91 speaks of finding security in God in our everyday life, as well as in the midst of any global, or personal, upheaval. Meditate on these psalms. "Mutter" them over to yourself. Consider the depths of their content. Find in them the place of trust and blessing now and forever.

For the LORD God is a sun and shield:

the LORD will give grace and glory:

no good thing will he withhold from them that walk uprightly.

O LORD of hosts, blessed is the man that trusteth in thee.

Psalm 84:11-12

BIBLIOGRAPHY

Aland, Kurt. *Martin Luther's 95 Theses.* Saint Louis: Concordia Publishing House, 1967.

"Birds of the Bible—Trusting under the Wing." *Lee's Birdwatching Adventures Plus Birdwatching from a Christian Perspective.* 9 January 2013, https://leesbird.com/2013/01/09/birds-of-the-bible-trusting-under-the-wing.

Crystal, David. *Begat: The King James Bible and the English Language.* Oxford: Oxford University Press, 2011.

"Dinosaur Questions and Answers." CREATION.com. 1 August 2018. https://creation.com/dinosaur-questions-and-answers.

Douglas, J.D. *The New Bible Dictionary.* Leicester, England: Inter-Varsity Press, 1978.

"G142 - airō - Strong's Greek Lexicon (mgnt)." Blue Letter Bible. Accessed 14 August 2023. https://www.blueletterbible.org/lexicon/g142/mgnt/tr/0-1.

Goard, Rev. W. Pascoe. *The Names of God.* Durham: The Covenant Publishing Co. Ltd., 2010.

Halley, John W. *Alleged Discrepancies of the Bible.* Springdale: Whitaker House, n.d.

Hammond, Peter. *The Greatest Century of Reformation.* Cape Town: Christian Liberty Books, 2006.

Hoad, T. F., ed. *Concise Oxford Dictionary of Word Origins, The.* Oxford: Oxford University Press, 1986.

Howley, G. C. D. *A New Testament Commentary.* London: Pickering & Inglis Ltd, 1969.

Jamieson, Robert, A. R. Fausset, and David Brown. *Commentary Critical and Explanatory on the Whole Bible.* Vol. 2. Oak Harbor, WA: Logos Research Systems, Inc., 1997.

Ken, Thomas. "Praise God From Whom All Blessings Flow." *Melodies of Praise.* Springfield: Gospel Publishing House, 1957. Public domain.

MacLaren, Alexander. "Psalm 2." Blue Letter Bible. Last Modified 15 April 2022. https://www.blueletterbible.org/comm/maclaren_alexander/the-expositors-bible/psalms-volume-one/psalm-two.cfm.

Moore, Thomas. "Come, Ye Disconsolate". 1046 Hymnals. https://hymnary.org/text/come_ye_disconsolate_whereer_ye_languish. Public domain.

Morgan, G. Campbell. *Great Chapters of the Bible.* Old Tappan: Fleming H Revell Co., 1935.

Nicholson, Adam. *Power and Glory: Jacobean England and the Making of the King James Bible.* London: Harper Collins Publishers, 2003.

"O.T. Names of God - Study Resources." Blue Letter Bible. Accessed 21 December, 2023. https://www.blueletterbible.org/study/misc/name_god.cfm.

Sedia, Adam. "The Power of One: Monosyllables in Classical Poetry." The Society of Classical Poets. 18 February, 2021. https://classicalpoets.org/2021/02/18/the-power-of-onemonosyllables-in-classical-poetry/#/%20.

Spurgeon, Charles. "Psalm 91 by C. H. Spurgeon." Blue Letter Bible. Last Modified 5 Dec 2016. https://www.blueletterbible.org/Comm/spurgeon_charles/tod/pso91.cfm.

Strong, James. *Strong's Expanded Exhaustive Concordance of the Bible.* Nashville: Thomas Nelson, 1990.

"Strong's G75 – agōnizomai." Blue Letter Bible. Accessed 21 December, 2023. https://www.blueletterbible.org/lexicon/g75/mgnt/tr/0-1/.

Studies in Christian Living, Book 5: Foundations for Faith. Christchurch: The Navigators, 1964.

Van Der Toorn, Karel. *Scribal Culture and the Making of the Hebrew Bible.* Cambridge, Massachusetts: Harvard University Press, 2007.

Vine, W.E. *An Expository Dictionary of New Testament Words*. Iowa Falls: Riverside Book and Bible House, 1952.

Wenham, Gordon. *The Psalter Reclaimed: Praying and Praising with the Psalms*. Wheaton, Illinois: Crossway, 2013.

Worgul, John E. "The Quatrain in Isaianic Poetry." *Grace Theological Journal* 11. No. 2 (1990): 187-204. https://biblicalstudies.org.uk/pdf/gtj/11-2_187.pdf.

ABOUT THE AUTHOR

GUY STEWARD HAS A teaching background in music, English, and art history. His writing career began with letters to the editor, articles, and, later, blogs. It finally came to fruition with his first book on cult mind control, published in 1998. In 2021, after twenty-five years in full-time teaching, his next book, *Living the Beatitudes Today*, and its study guide were published by Ambassador International. Guy is also a musician and an occasional composer and has performed recitals on the classical guitar.

For more information about

Guy Robert Peel Steward
and
A Harmony of Two Psalms
please visit:

www.guysteward.com

Ambassador International's mission is to magnify the Lord Jesus Christ and promote His gospel through the written word.

We believe through the publication of Christian literature, Jesus Christ and His Word will be exalted, believers will be strengthened in their walk with Him, and the lost will be directed to Jesus Christ as the only way of salvation.

For more information about
AMBASSADOR INTERNATIONAL
please visit:

www.ambassador-international.com
@AmbassadorIntl
www.facebook.com/AmbassadorIntl

Thank you for reading this book. Please consider leaving us a review on your social media, favorite retailer's website, Goodreads or Bookbub, or our website.

www.ingramcontent.com/pod-product-compliance
Lightning Source LLC
Chambersburg PA
CBHW060514090426
42735CB00011B/2215